Photoshop® for Right-Brainers

Third Edition

Photoshop® for Right-Brainers

The Art of Photo Manipulation

Third Edition

Al Ward

WILEY

Wiley Publishing, Inc.

Acquisitions Editor: Mariann Barsolo
Development Editor: Thomas Cirtin
Technical Editor: Doug Nelson
Production Editor: Melissa Lopez
Copy Editors: Elizabeth Welch and Linda Recktenwald
Production Manager: Tim Tate
Vice President and Executive Group Publisher: Richard Swadley
Vice President and Publisher: Neil Edde
Media Project Supervisor: Laura Moss-Hollister
Media Development Specialist: Josh Frank
Media Quality Assurance: Angie Denny
Compositors: Chris Gillespie and Maureen Forys, Happenstance Type-O-Rama
Proofreader: Candace English
Indexer: Ted Laux
Cover Designer: Nadia Chung, winner of the 2008 Wiley Design Challenge

Library of Congress Cataloging-in-Publication Data

Ward, Al.
  Photoshop for right-brainers : the art of photo manipulation / Al Ward. — 3rd ed.
    p. cm.
  ISBN-13: 978-0-470-39701-5 (paper/CD-ROM)
  ISBN-10: 0-470-39701-2 (paper/CD-ROM)
  1. Computer graphics. 2. Adobe Photoshop. 3. Photography—Digital techniques. 4. Photography—Retouching—Data processing. I. Title.

  T385.W369 2009
  006.6'86—dc22
                    2008052148

Dear Reader,

Thank you for choosing *Photoshop for Right-Brainers: The Art of Photo Manipulation, 3rd Edition*. This book is part of a family of premium-quality Sybex books, all of which are written by outstanding authors who combine practical experience with a gift for teaching.

Sybex was founded in 1976. More than thirty years later, we're still committed to producing consistently exceptional books. With each of our titles we're working hard to set a new standard for the industry. From the paper we print on, to the authors we work with, our goal is to bring you the best books available.

I hope you see all that reflected in these pages. I'd be very interested to hear your comments and get your feedback on how we're doing. Feel free to let me know what you think about this or any other Sybex book by sending me an email at nedde@wiley.com, or if you think you've found a technical error in this book, please visit `http://sybex.custhelp.com`. Customer feedback is critical to our efforts at Sybex.

Best regards,

Neil Edde
Vice President and Publisher
Sybex, an Imprint of Wiley

I dedicate this book to Tonia, Noah, and Ali.

Acknowledgments

As with every book I write, I find writing this section to be the most difficult. There are so many good, hardworking people behind a book project such as this that some invariably fall through the cracks. Not to mention loved ones, friends, and influential people whom I relate to or who have been an integral part of my life and thus affect my thought process... there are far too many to mention but who deserve to be acknowledged in this section. If anyone reading this feels you should have been included but fails to see your name here, consider yourself included.

I have to start with my wife Tonia and my children Noah and Ali. They are the reason I get out of bed in the morning and the joy in my life. Without them I'd be truly lost and alone... with them I'm complete. What else can I say? I love you all dearly.

Special thanks to Mariann, Tom, Pete, Kelly, and the entire team at Sybex. I appreciate your hard work, your faith in me, and definitely your patience during this project. Life threw a few curves during the course of this book, but you managed to get me back on track when needed and made this project a joy.

Thanks to Melissa Lopez and the production team at Wiley, who expertly put the words and images into the pages found here.

I cannot express enough my thanks to my good friend Kim Smith. Kim took over a lot of the day-to-day managing of my forum, helped with my website advertising, and cracked the whip when I fell behind in my various projects... all with patience and a smile. I've never met Kim in person, but I feel we've been great friends for a long, long time. Thanks again, Kim... I don't simply appreciate the things you do, but I appreciate *you*. Say "hi" to your parents for me.

Thanks to my good friend and fellow designer/author Colin Smith. No matter how often my wife tries to get him married off, he still keeps accepting our calls and coming to visit. Now that's friendship!

I can't thank Colin without also mentioning his website (www.photoshopcafe.com) and all the people who find solace in the forum there. PhotoshopCAFE has developed into a great source of inspiration and friendship where Photoshop users of all stripes can find acceptance. The coffee is always hot and fresh; I'll see you there.

To Richard Lynch, a good friend (and an excellent author/teacher) and trusted sounding board when I need him most. You need to head out west one of these days and pay me a visit. Thanks, buddy!

To the people who know my work and keep coming back anyway; those who both visit and join my website (www.actionfx.com). If you keep visiting, I'll keep working to make your life in Photoshop a bit easier, fun, and hopefully profitable.

To Mom, Dad, Ole, Linda, and my extended family (I'm from Montana, so there are hundreds of people who qualify for this): I love you all, in spite of the restraining order. (Just kidding... I had it lifted so you can visit again.)

To my dear friends at the Missoula Landmark Missionary Baptist Church: Pastor Mike and Vicki Maney; Pastor Phil, Deborah, Rachel, and Zion Maney; Scott and Lana Weeks; Andrew, Hannah, Asher, and Lydia Maney (and the wee one on the way as of this writing); and again my in-laws Ole and Linda Field, my wife and children. We walk the same road, and I'm honored to share it with you.

The greatest thanks and highest praise go to my God and Savior, without whom none of this would be possible or worthwhile. He saw fit to allow this Montana boy to realize his dream.

Again, if I forgot anyone who really needed to be here, please forgive me and consider yourself included. To all my readers and friends far and wide, my deepest regards and a hearty thank-you from the bottom of my heart.

About the Author

Al Ward is a prominent figure in the Photoshop community. His website, www.actionfx.com, supplies Photoshop actions, Photoshop presets, digital-scrapbooking embellishments, and video training and information to users. He has written and contributed to numerous Photoshop books, including *Photoshop Most Wanted* and *Photoshop Most Wanted 2* (with Colin Smith), *Photoshop CS3 Type Effects Gone Wild*, *Al Ward's Photoshop Productivity Toolkit*, *Photoshop Elements 2 Special Effects*, and *Photoshop 7 Effects Magic.* He has written for Planet Photoshop, PhotoshopCAFE, Graphics.com, and *Photoshop User* magazine, as well as many other articles in print and online.

Contents

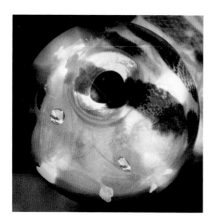

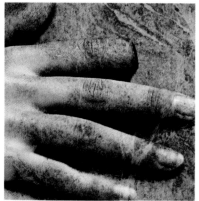

Introduction

Photoshop for Right-Brainers : The Art of Photo Manipulation, 3rd Edition, is a guide to using Photoshop CS4's toolkit to unlock your own creativity, as I've used it to unlock mine. The Pause button in my brain evidently ceased working from overuse during my Navy days, and now there is no stopping the cartoons, dramas, and horror movies broadcasting in my head. I'll wake on occasion with some incredible insight and be overcome with an urge to share this unrefined gem of intellectual acrobatics with my wife. She can barely contain her joy; you can see it in the way she smiles, nods, and says, "Would you like bacon for breakfast?" or "Stop jumping around and talking nonsense or you'll scare the kids!"

For me, Photoshop CS4, as well as every other incarnation since Photoshop 4 sooooo many years ago, has opened pathways for creativity that I had always known were in my head but that I had no way to translate to the real world. What originally attracted me to the program was not the capability to correct photographs but the power to warp photographs into something else. This journey started as an experiment in creating something from nothing (I think the first effect that I tried to master was creating fire from thin air) and developed into a career based on corrections, distortions, and manipulations. Photoshop gives me the ability to take the critters in my head and make them a visual reality. Teaching the program and writing about those discoveries was an unexpected, but extremely appreciated, bonus. It's sort of like writing a great (or even mediocre) novel; the novelist doesn't simply shelve the reams of paper to read to himself from time to time but rather tries to put the book into print so others can appreciate the story. Photoshop is my typewriter, and the entities and scenes that form on my screen are the novel. I share it in hopes that someone out there in the big old world will appreciate it. More often than not people do; occasionally I'll get an email asking me if I want bacon for breakfast. Some folks are just odd.

Why I Wrote This Book

When I approached the first edition of *Photoshop for Right-Brainers,* I wanted to do something a bit different from what I've written in the past. I certainly did not want to write another "These are the basics of Adobe Photoshop" book; there are many authors out there who have done an excellent job tackling that subject. I also did not want to simply create a recipe book of canned effects. I've done that before, and while recipe books have their place, I wanted this book, now in its third edition, to be a bit more personal. Don't get me wrong—this book is full of effects that you can follow along with and implement. What I want the reader to see, aside from the step-by-step process, is how I develop ideas for projects. Where do the concepts for the various effects come from? When an idea is pieced together in the imagination, what does it look like? And last, what tools in Adobe Photoshop CS4 can be used to make those scenes or creatures take on new life on the computer?

Right Brain? Left Brain?

About 30 years ago, the artist and educator Betty Edwards wrote a book that has become a classic and that is indirectly an inspiration for this one: *Drawing on the Right Side of the Brain*. At that time, it wasn't widely understood by the general public that the right and left hemispheres of the brain function differently and control different kinds of intelligence, so Edwards devoted a chapter to explaining her premise: The left side is logical, analytical, sequential, and verbal, and it tends to break things down into parts rather than look at wholes. The right side is intuitive, synthesizing, spatial, and holistic. It is, in short, the source of visual imagination and creativity. Today, that understanding is much more widespread, to the point where *right-brained* and *left-brained* have become a kind of shorthand for different ways of looking at the world.

My book, although targeted at right-brained designers and photographers, is not simply for them. I suspect that more than a few left-brained people (who I affectionately call *lefties*) are really closet right-brained people, waiting for someone to lead the way past their math, science, and politics and into the realm of artistic expression. My aim is not that the content appeal to only the right-brained crowd. Rather, I hope that the book may also serve in some small way as a beacon that guides lefties through the dismal smog of facts and figures and into the Technicolor world that righties have lived in and appreciated for generations. Even a lefty can be a right-brainer; the world could use a few creative politicians, after all.

What Should You Know Already?

Photoshop users are generally lumped into three main categories (not my doing): beginner, intermediate, and advanced. This tends to paint Photoshop users with an extremely broad brush, not taking into account the many genres of digital manipulation for which Photoshop is used. For instance, a person can be exceptional at special effects but not have the slightest clue about how images are prepared for print.

In general terms, a person hoping to get the most from this book should at least be intermediate in his understanding of and experience with the software. By *intermediate,* I simply mean you should have used the tools, be familiar with the interface, have a concept of how layers work, and so forth. Since Photoshop CS4 has altered a few things from previous incarnations (panels instead of palettes, for instance), you may want to spend some time becoming familiar with the interface and terms used. The Help files will help you immensely here. You should also be familiar with following tutorial-style instructions. If you have just purchased the software and have absolutely no clue what a pixel is, then you should probably pass on this book for now and come back to it after trying something a bit more introductory. If you have some experience with the program and have a keen desire to try things in new and interesting ways, then this is the book for you.

How the Book Is Organized

The book is organized in what I call a progressive format. That is to say, the chapters are complete unto themselves, but later chapters refer to and/or include techniques used in earlier chapters. As a result, the earlier chapters serve as building blocks for what you will see later. This helps avoid reviewing a series of commands multiple times, allowing space for more techniques.

Chapter 1, "Tools for Building Your Masterpiece," focuses on the most important tools and concepts underlying the techniques you'll explore throughout the book: blending modes, layer masks, adjustment layers, Blend If, removing subjects from their backgrounds, and displacement maps.

Chapter 2, "Techniques for Embellishing Portraits," presents basic and advanced cosmetic corrections and enhancements that portrait subjects may often request, such as deepening (or completely changing) eye color, covering up old acne scars, and the like. Why stop there? This chapter also covers radical techniques for more-dramatic changes, such as digital liposuction and face-lifts.

Chapter 3, "A Few Right-Brained Special Effects," ventures into the realm of special effects—that is to say, techniques for art creation that are not specifically photo-related. This chapter looks at the creation of glass spheres, chrome objects, plastic—I even show you how to turn your photos into unique Victorian-style seamless patterns.

Chapter 4, "Texture, Color, and Layer Effects," explores a few tools and techniques that will enhance the art of any designer and help you achieve those tricky, elusive results you have been looking for. Apply Image is demonstrated, and you will also learn to add color to black-and-white images, apply textures by using displacement maps, and even enhance old paintings by using common Photoshop tools.

Chapter 5, "Effects in the Real World," leads you through transforming natural and human-made forms. You'll mirror rock formations, create neon reflections on rainy streets, and turn sunny landscapes into nightmare scenes.

Chapter 6, "Animals," continues the theme of transformations as you add human features to animals and vice versa, create a Pegasus, and more.

Chapter 7, "Digital Alterations and Manipulations," ventures into the realm of graphic arts: digital manipulation for use in advertising, macro-enhancement, and other interesting areas.

Chapter 8, "Going Beyond Canned Filters," works with a Photoshop feature that is often misused. The projects here show that applying a filter should be a starting point, not a finished product. For example, you'll "age" a new photograph for a retro effect, turn photographs into line drawings, and work to make dynamic brushes for use in your work.

Chapter 9, "People as Art: Digital Manipulation," treats the human body as a canvas. You will color it, texture it, melt it, and mold it—painting a checkered flag onto a swimsuit model and turning flesh into stone.

Chapter 10, "Digital Intensive: Fast and Furious Projects," takes bits of techniques learned throughout the book and utilizes them in completely different ways. You'll learn to create photorealistic digital frames for your photos, turn your pictures into all manner of Photoshop presets for use in other projects or for distribution, and use some lighting and coloring tricks to generate your very own monster.

Appendix A, "Accessing Additional Resources," provides some helpful links and resources for you to explore more right-brained worlds.

Appendix B, "About the Companion CD" provides more useful information about the accompanying CD.

Using the CD Files

The images used in this book are also provided for your use on the accompanying CD. Some were taken by the author, but the majority are provided by Photos.com. Please note that these photos are for your use with this book only; they are not in the public domain and may not be redistributed in any way, shape, or form.

At each point where you need to use a file from the CD in order to work through an exercise, you'll see a symbol in the margin like the one shown here, and the text will refer to the specific filename. That way, you'll use the same images as I did when completing an exercise

Feedback

Both the author and the publisher encourage you to offer feedback on this text. Was it useful to you? What did you learn that you did not know previously? You may leave your comments with the publisher at www.sybex.com or send the author a note through his website at www.actionfx.com.

Go to www.sybex.com/go/rightbrainers for future updates to the book's content.

Photoshop® for Right-Brainers

Third Edition

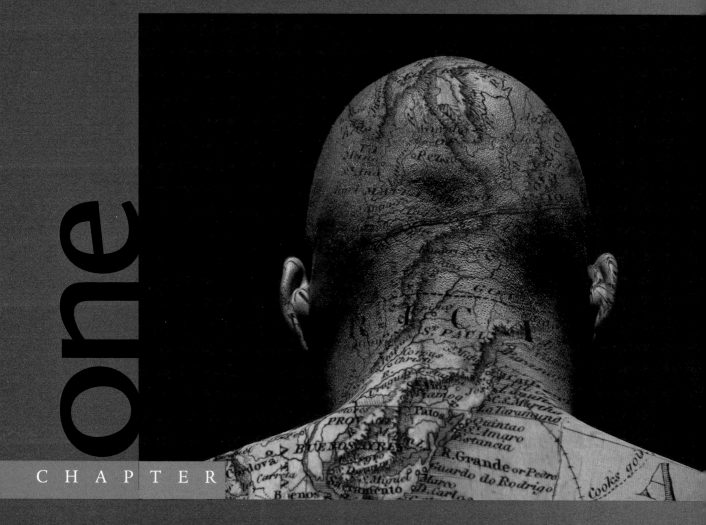

one

Tools for Building Your Masterpiece

Right-brainers are typically artistic *in some fashion, and this book is for people who, like me, enjoy the journey. Although right-brainers are constantly chiding left-brained people to think outside the proverbial box, a right-brainer who works with a piece of software such as Adobe Photoshop CS4 needs to spend some time in the box, getting to know the tools and techniques that will lead to masterpieces at some future date.*

This chapter discusses a few of the most important techniques and tools that are used throughout the book, as well as some that are just plain good to know: blending modes, extractions, layer masks, those all-powerful adjustment layers (made even more powerful in CS4 than in earlier releases), displacement maps, and the Blend If feature. I can't teach you to be an artist, but I certainly can show you some of the tools I use that you might find helpful in your own work. Let's take a look at some of these key techniques.

The images referenced as source files for these techniques can be found in the Chapter 1 Source Files *folder on this book's CD.*

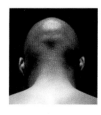

Using Blending Modes

For right-brainers, blending modes open entirely new doors that perhaps you haven't considered. For example, you can quickly collage two images by placing them in layers and experimenting with the blending modes for just the right mix.

Blending modes for layers simply tell Photoshop how the pixels in one layer will interact with the pixels in the layers beneath. You knew that already, though, right? Sure you did; at least, you probably already know if you have spent any time with Photoshop. As you work through the next few chapters, you'll use various blending modes. For each new mode that's introduced, you'll find a short definition.

Instead of rambling on about how you *should* use them, I'll show a few examples of how you *can* use them to your advantage.

Blending Landscapes

From this book's CD-ROM, open the images `mesa.jpg` and `sunset.jpg` (see Figures 1.1 and 1.2). Here you have two images of similar tone and theme. You might consider what these two photos would look like merged. To check that out, have one photo serve as the foundation image, and paste the other photo into a new layer in that document (see Figure 1.3).

Each blending mode, when applied to the sunset layer, will give a different result. You might think that the Overlay mode would produce a good mix of the two images, so check it out! Figure 1.4 shows the image with the sunset layer set to Overlay.

Personally I love the results of this blend: the addition of the clouds and color variation to the mesa's backdrop is simply stunning. This wouldn't be much of an experiment if we stopped here, however.

Figure 1.1 Choose images to blend together. Here's the first image.

Figure 1.2 The second image

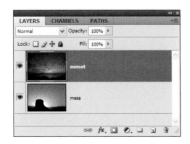

Figure 1.3 Place both images into the same document for merging.

Figure 1.4 *Sunset layer blending mode set to Overlay*

Experimenting with Blending Modes

Try another test, this time selecting Darken for the blending mode of the sunset layer (see Figure 1.5). This results in a very deep melding of the two images. The outline of the mesa is clearly defined still, but we see more characteristics and features of the sunset layer. The primary thing that strikes me as being wrong with this version is it is simply too dark. It makes sense: the sunset layer is in Darken mode, so those areas that are darker than the layer beneath will be darkened. Those lighter will not. The clouds are better defined, but we lose the bright appeal of the previous example.

Let's give it another shot. Follow along and see what you come up with. Change the blending mode for the sunset layer to Soft Light (see Figure 1.6). That is a good mix for achieving definition between the two photos. The colors are less harsh, and we still have good definition in both the mesa and the clouds.

Figure 1.5 *Sunset layer in Darken blending mode*

Figure 1.6 *Another version using Soft Light blending mode*

The Soft Light blending mode takes a look at the blend color and either lightens or darkens that portion of the image, depending on whether the color is lighter or darker, respectively, than 50% gray. If the light source, or blend color, is lighter than 50% gray, the effect is as though that portion of the image were dodged—darker makes it look as though it were burned. Painting with Black or White in the Soft Light blending mode will darken or lighten, but will not result in true black or white. Rather, it will result in an increase of light or shadow.

When you find a blending mode that does basically what you want it to accomplish, as I've done with this example, you may want to keep the blending mode and finish the corrections with other Photoshop features. No one tool or technique is a cure-all: it usually takes a combination of tools and commands working together to get what you are looking for.

Notice the jet stream trailing off in the upper-left corner. This can be wiped away to help maintain the Old West feel of the final shot. One of the quickest ways to isolate and replace the offending area is to use the Spot Healing tool on the mesa layer (see Figure 1.7). Figure 1.8 shows out final blended image.

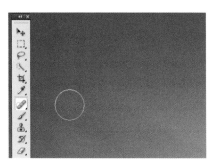

Figure 1.7 *Spot Healing quickly replaces the offending jet stream with the blue background surrounding the aircraft.*

Figure 1.8 Final blended image

As you work through the book, blending modes will become second nature. What I want you to take away from these brief examples, in particular for merging layers, is that your choice of blending mode will dictate whether a piece fails or succeeds. You have many to choose from, but usually one or two come close. You want to get to the point where you intuitively know what additional tools in conjunction with the blending mode will give you the results you are looking for. Photoshop isn't out to get you: it is only as smart and creative as you allow it to be. Photoshop is the toolbox; you are the artist.

Extracting an Image from a Background

I belong to several Photoshop-related forums and lists online (a favorite hangout of mine is PhotoshopCAFE at www.photoshopcafe.com), and it amazes me how many posts start with the heading "How do I extract an image from a background?" Indeed, Photoshop doesn't give the casual user an easy answer, as there is a number of ways to perform this very task. The best method for the task depends on a couple of factors: the job at hand (the object being extracted, the background the object resides in) and the user's knowledge of the software or preferred method.

If the background is a solid color, you can use the Background Eraser tool with passable results, but many in the graphics world consider this approach to be cheating in some way. If it works, I say go for it, but rarely does that method work to satisfaction.

In the previous editions of this book, I demonstrated how to perform extractions using the Extract feature, which as of this writing has been removed for Adobe Photoshop CS4. I'm mixing things up a bit with this update, and will instead demonstrate extracting objects or subjects using the Pen tool.

Removing Objects from Their Background

 Let's get started and remove an object from its background. Open the image `apple.jpg` from this book's CD (see Figure 1.9).

Let's pull the apple off the background and give it a new home. Duplicate the Background layer. Create a new layer between the two apple layers and fill it with white. Rename the Background Copy **Extract** (see Figure 1.10).

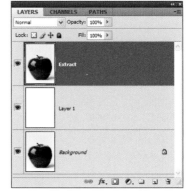

Figure 1.9 *The apple will serve as our extraction model.*

Figure 1.10 *Set up the Layers panel for extracting.*

Select the Pen tool in the Toolbar. On the Options bar click the Paths icon; it is the second icon from the left at the top of the screen (see Figure 1.11). Click the mouse anywhere along the edge of the subject (in this case, the apple) to serve as a starting point. Move along the edge of the object a short distance in either direction and click to add another point. If the path between the two points rests on a curve on the object's edge, hold down the mouse when you create the second point and drag it further along the edge a short distance. This will cause the straight path to slowly conform to the curve of the apple's edge.

Figure 1.11 *Creating a path can be tricky but gets easier with practice.*

Work your way around the entire apple, including the stem. You may have to exercise a little guesswork in the areas of extreme highlight or shadow, so work the path to make the shape appear natural. When you have reached the starting point, click on the first point to close the path (see Figure 1.12).

After you have outlined the entire apple, open the Paths panel. You will see a new Work Path resident in the shape of your apple (see Figure 1.13). The next step is to convert the path into a selection, which you do by clicking the Load Path As A Selection icon at the bottom of the Paths panel (the third icon from the left) or by opening the Paths panel menu and selecting Make Selection from the list (see Figure 1.14).

Once the "marching ants" appear around the apple, you can copy the apple and paste it into a new document for later use. To copy the apple, press ⌘/Ctrl+C or select Edit → Copy. Create a new document (File → New or ⌘/Ctrl+N), which will be the size of the apple by default. Ensure the Background is set to Transparent to avoid having to extract the apple again in the future in case you save it in a nonlayered format (see Figure 1.15).

Figure 1.12 *After working the path around the object, click the starting point to close the path.*

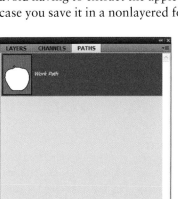

Figure 1.13 *The new path resides in the Paths panel.*

Figure 1.14 *Convert the path into a selection.*

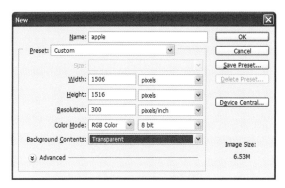

Figure 1.15 *When you copy the object and create a new document to place it in, by default the new document fits the dimensions of the object.*

Paste the apple into the new document (⌘/Ctrl+V; see Figure 1.16). If you would like to save this image for later use, I recommend saving it as a PNG file. This format will retain the transparent background so you can easily drag and drop the object into any photo environment you choose as well as resize it to fit your needs.

Figure 1.16 *The apple in a new transparent background*

Have you ever created a new document with a transparent background and find it appears all white? Where are the tiny gray squares that we all know and love? The checker pattern expected to delineate transparency is actually still there. Photoshop CS4 at times defaults to a variation of light gray/dark gray squares so it is difficult to see that the document background is indeed transparent. To change this, select Edit → Preferences → Transparency And Gamut; Mac users will find Preferences under the Photoshop menu. From here, you can change the color of the squares simply by clicking on one (there are two shown) and selecting a slightly darker shade of gray. Now your transparent backgrounds will have the little alternating checkers once again.

A New Home

The true test comes when you try placing your object in a new setting. Take a look at Figure 1.17. What if we replace the eight ball with the newly extracted apple? To play along, open the `eightball.jpg` image found on the book's CD. With the newly extracted apple image open (the one resting on the transparent background), drag and drop the apple into the eight ball file and place the apple over the pool ball with either the Move tool or the arrow keys (see Figure 1.18). The Move tool needs to be selected in order for the arrow keys to work.

Figure 1.17 *Eight ball, corner pocket*

Figure 1.18 *The apple in a new environment*

Choose Edit → Transform → Scale and resize the apple to better conform to the size of the eight ball without leaving any of the ball showing (see Figure 1.19). Once it's in place, accept the transformation.

You may want to use the Burn tool to darken the lower edge of the apple as well as the ground beneath it to better conform it to the image. You may also add a shadow to the grass with the Burn tool to achieve a bit more realism (see Figure 1.20).

Figure 1.19 *Resize as needed.*

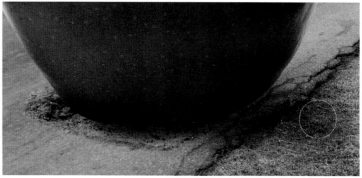

Figure 1.20 *Shadowing with the Burn tool*

Figure 1.21 *Create a feathered selection.*

Let's do one more little trick before we move on. As the apple leaves a shadow on the grass, the grass in turn should leave a reflection on the apple. We can simulate this by generating a feathered selection on the right side of the apple with the Lasso tool, then creating a Hue/Saturation adjustment layer and forcing a green tonal change to that area.

To see what I mean, select the Lasso tool. On the Options bar change the Feather radius to 20px. Draw a selection along the lower-right region of the apple's edge, as seen in Figure 1.21. You can move the selection into place with the arrow keys so the selection roughly follows along the edge of the object.

At the bottom of the Layers panel, click the Create New Fill Or Adjustment Layer icon. Choose Hue/Saturation from the menu. Any adjustments will be focused on the selected area thanks to the adjustment layer's mask (see Figure 1.22).

New in Photoshop CS4 are the Adjustments and Masks panels, which give you more control over the adjustments made and the areas of the layer affected.

With the adjustment layer in place, double-click it in the Layers panel to open the Adjustments panel. Move the Hue slider until you get a subtle green reflection (see Figure 1.23). Once the adjustment is made, you should have replaced the eight ball with the apple, complete with enhanced shadows and colored reflection (see Figure 1.24).

Figure 1.22 *The mask helps isolate a region to be corrected or edited.*

Figure 1.23 *The Adjustments panel gives you great control over your edits.*

Figure 1.24 *The apple in its new home*

Granted, the final image is a bit "far out," but the extraction itself worked like a charm. The Path tool does take a bit of practice, but there is nothing like it for giving you crisp, clear edges for your extracted objects.

Working with Layer Masks

As you delve into all the nifty things Photoshop allows you to do to your images, you may have already played a bit with layer masks. Layer masks, at their most basic, are simple bit-maps attached to a layer. The black in the bitmap, or mask, hides the pixels of the standard layer, and the white reveals those pixels.

As mentioned in the previous section, Photoshop CS4 has added a Masks panel that allows you to control density, feather, color range, and other mask features. We will be looking at these features throughout the book.

First, let's look at some possible uses of masks. What benefit do you see from being able to hide portions of a layer? Here's one practical application using two layers with the same pixel information: you could correct the top layer or do some fancy special effect to it and then mask away portions of the layer so the correction or effect seems to occur only on certain portions of the image. Layer masks are also excellent for merging photos, either gradually or starkly, so collages are a breeze. Masks even go so far as to allow a savvy right-brainer to turn any photograph into a seamless pattern or a floor tile.

Let me demonstrate what I'm talking about.

Dynamic Masking

I'll begin with a practical example. If you have perused any medium to large electronics store online, in particular those that sell mid- to high-end televisions or computers, you may have noted that many display their products with an image on the screen. It is difficult to take a photograph of a television with the screen active and have it turn out with ad-quality resolution on the display. Rather than leave the screen blank, many retailers will use Photoshop to place an image on the screen to make the product shot more compelling. Layer masks can achieve this goal in quick order.

Figure 1.25 A standard computer-monitor product shot

 For this example, open monitor.jpg (Figure 1.25) and tech.jpg (Figure 1.26).

Figure 1.26 A techno-collage to fill the screen

To see how masks can help when working with these two images, you first need to place them in the same document. To do this, simply copy the second photo and paste it into the first. They are different sizes, so choose Edit → Transform → Scale and resize the new layer to match the size of the first. In this instance, you need to be concerned only that the monitor screen is overlaid with the second image (see Figure 1.27).

When working with a lot of layers, it is smart to give your layers descriptive names. You're working with only two layers in this example, but it is still a good habit to establish, so rename the layers **Monitor** (the base layer) and **Tech**. The top layer is where the masking will take place; you can create that mask now by selecting the Tech layer and clicking the Add Layer Mask icon at the bottom of the Layers panel (see Figure 1.28).

Figure 1.27 *Transform the top layer to match the monitor screen size.*

Figure 1.28 *Renaming layers can help organize your edits.*

As a demonstration of how masks help in this instance, you can quickly place the techno-collage on the monitor without overlapping beyond the screen's border. This is a piece of cake because the monitor face is roughly the same color across the object.

There are a few tools you can use to generate a selection of the screen. The Polygonal Lasso and Magnetic Lasso tools are safe bets, and even using the Select → Color Range dialog box would provide moderate success. Looking at the monitor, with its clear, concise edges on the border of the screen, you might see that the quickest and easiest way to generate the needed selection most likely resides in the Magic Wand tool and its default settings. Ensure that the Monitor layer is active in the Layers panel and use the Magic Wand to generate your selection by clicking directly on the screen. If the entire screen doesn't select, increase the Tolerance value in the Options bar to 40 or so (see Figure 1.29).

When the selection is generated, return to the Tech layer and create the mask. The black in the mask hides the portions of the layer outside the screen area, while the white area in the mask reveals the Tech layer. The effect is that the image is now displayed on the screen, as you can see in Figure 1.30.

Figure 1.29 *Generating a selection of the area where the second image will be applied will help you quickly place the photo in the next step.*

Figure 1.30 *The only area in the mask that should be filled with white is the monitor screen.*

If you have performed the masking technique properly, you will have a final product image with the Tech image resident only on the monitor. Any additional corrections to the mask that may be required can be performed by using the paint tools with either white or black to correct and clean up areas of the masked layer (see Figure 1.31).

Figure 1.31 *Final product shot with screen image in place*

Absurd Symmetry

For the digital artist, masks are frequently used to generate symmetry in a photo or working piece of art. Photographers may use masks for fine-tuning the appearance of a model; a wacky right-brainer may take things to the extreme and use one photo to create a perfect, albeit improbable, vision of beauty. Figure 1.32 (`ModelShot.jpg` on the CD) shows a young lady who has absolutely nothing wrong with her. Well, in the real world maybe. In the digital world, however, we can use Photoshop to give perfect symmetry. In other words, Photoshop masks can be utilized in such a way as to make the right side of the face the exact, if mirror opposite, twin of the left.

Let's see what a mask can do to enhance this photo. With a photo open in Photoshop, duplicate the Background layer. Name both layers accordingly: in this example name the layers **Model-01** for the foundation and **Model-02** for the layer to be manipulated with the mask. With the Model-02 layer selected, choose Edit → Transform → Flip Horizontal to rotate the image, and then click the Add Layer Mask icon at the bottom of the Layers panel (see Figure 1.33). By drawing a standard Black to White gradient across the mask and using the default settings (that is, a gradual change from black to white), you'll see the photo take on characteristics of both layers (see Figure 1.34). The condition of the layer mask at this stage can be seen in Figure 1.35.

Figure 1.33 *Model-02 layer flipped and the mask firmly in place*

Figure 1.32 *I'm ready for my close-up.*

Figure 1.34 *A standard Black to White gradient in the mask gives the model a surreal appearance.*

Figure 1.35 *The Layers panel should look like this in this step.*

The result is interesting but we can make it more so by shortening the length of the gradient to a very small area in the center of the photo rather than across the entire image. For instance, redraw the same gradient in the same mask, but this time span the width of the mouth (Figure 1.36). The result has less faded blending and gives the model the appearance of being a computer-generated female in some 3D rendering program rather than a living, breathing human (see Figure 1.37).

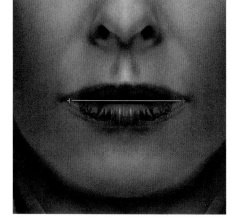

Figure 1.36 *Narrowing the distance between the Black and White color stops in the gradient eliminates much of the transparency effect, restricting it to a narrow area.*

Reversing the colors in the mask creates an entirely different rendition of the model, though in this case it tends to make her look a bit masculine (see Figure 1.38). This can be altered by moving the top layer toward the right to "pinch" her face and neck back to a more feminine appearance. You may then use the paint brush on the Layer Mask, alternating with black, white, and shades of gray, to remove or enhance certain areas such as hair, the clothing, the neckline, and so forth (see Figure 1.39). The end result will still appear a bit "out of this world," but you get the point. This is simply an exercise in masking... and it does create some pretty interesting results!

Figure 1.37 *CGI... without rendering it in a 3D program*

Figure 1.38 *A more realistic marriage of layers*

Figure 1.39 *More mask manipulations*

Shades of Gray

One final example demonstrates how shades of gray can be used in a mask to create character in your collages or backgrounds (see Figure 1.40). In this instance, I've taken `tech-02.jpg` and `tech-03.jpg`, and placed them in new layers in the file `circuit.jpg`. Grayed masks (or layer masks filled with gray) have been applied to the top two layers.

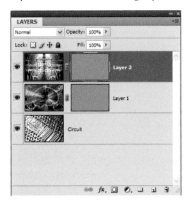

Figure 1.40 Using gray tones in a mask is a fast and easy way to create collages or to generate backgrounds with elements from multiple images.

When you look at the image with a mask applied, you'll see elements of both photos overlaying the original (see Figure 1.41). Basically this is the same effect as if you were reducing opacity or altering blending modes; however, you can use this effect in conjunction with opacity changes and blending-mode changes for variations you may not expect. I have said that before, I will say this now, and I promise I will say it again: experiment! You'll never know the effects you could have created unless you try subtly (or extremely, for that matter) altering settings in your images dreamed up by you. I can show you only a couple of variations in a few pages, but I really want you to explore your own creativity by using the tools at your disposal.

I will go deeper in detail concerning the new masking features as you proceed through the book. With such a powerful tool, you will have incredible digital art in short order.

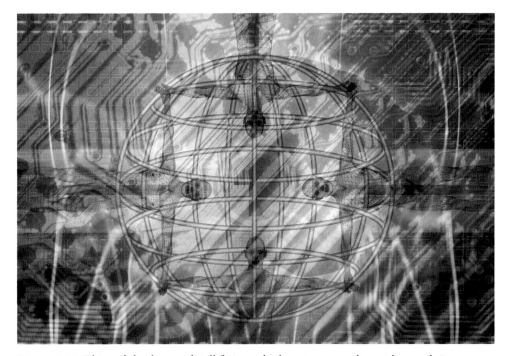

Figure 1.41 This tech background will fit in with almost any trendy, modern website.

Including Adjustment Layers

Something I have found to be incredibly useful for the past few versions of Photoshop was the inclusion of adjustment layers. Because of my interest in adding a personal touch to perfectly good photos, the final image often doesn't resemble the original except in passing. A long, long time ago, say three or four versions of Photoshop in the past, altering layer information was almost always "destructive." The actual pixels were altered, which could be troublesome if you forgot to save the original photo.

Adjustment layers have taken this concern, wrestled it to the floor, and given it a much-needed wedgie. You can now make adjustments to an entire image or aspects of certain layers without worrying about destroying the original document. You can always backtrack in the history, providing you remembered to take snapshots along the way. Who has time for snapshots? Bah, humbug!

Adjustment layers work simply by creating a new layer, separate from the other layers, that will let you make your tweaks. Each adjustment layer has a mask attached so that you can "paint away" the adjustments from areas of the image where you don't want them to apply. New to Photoshop CS4 is the ability to alter the mask density, isolate colors, and even feather and further refine the mask. You can alter the mask, and thereby the adjustment layer, by painting with black, white, or gray in the mask itself. Better yet, you can go back at any time, reopen the adjustment layer, and change the settings as you like—a particularly easy task with Photoshop CS4's new Adjustments panel. Adjustment layers each have the appropriate adjustment's dialog box attached. If you adjust levels by using a Levels adjustment layer, you do so the same way you do a standard Levels adjustment. The only difference is that you are making the changes to a nondestructive layer as opposed to actual pixels.

Correcting without Corrupting

To demonstrate correcting or editing an image in a non-destructive manner, or in such a way that the original pixels are not altered, I have chosen an image reflecting the theme of this book: a model of the human brain. Open the image `RightBrain.jpg` (see Figure 1.42).

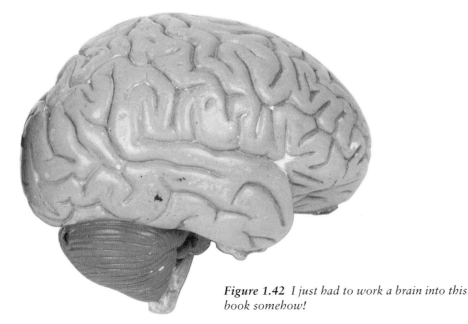

Figure 1.42 *I just had to work a brain into this book somehow!*

With the image open, click the Create New Fill Or Adjustment Layer icon at the bottom of the Layers panel. A menu will appear with a series of selections representing the types of adjustments you can make.

Choose Levels from the menu. A Levels adjustment layer will appear in the Layers panel (see Figure 1.43).

Select the Levels adjustments, and the Adjustments panel will change to give you a standard levels layout; you can make your Levels adjustment as you would if you were operating from the Image → Adjustments → Levels dialog box. Figure 1.44 shows a standard adjustment, moving the left slider to where the color information begins. Click OK to accept the adjustment.

I use this particular adjustment to darken the washed-out area of the brain, in particular the pink fleshy parts. I'm not sure that I want to adjust the gray area. By painting in the white mask with a black brush, you can wipe away the adjustment to that area, leaving the rest of the brain corrected (see Figure 1.45).

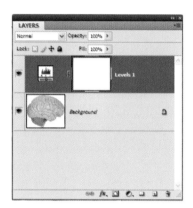

Figure 1.43 *The Levels adjustment layer is in position and ready to go to work.*

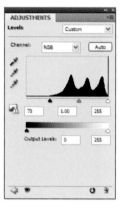

Figure 1.44 *Levels are adjusted in the standard way.*

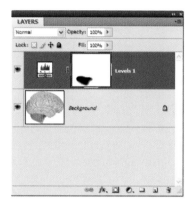

Figure 1.45 *Use the paint tools to mask areas you do not want to be altered by the adjustment layer.*

Let's say you would like to create a mock-up of this brain for a presentation of some sort. You have found the gray just doesn't cut it, and the brain seems flat on the projector. It's time for a color overhaul. By adding a Hue/Saturation adjustment layer that effectively colors the entire brain blue (see Figure 1.46) but then hiding most of the image except those areas you want to have colored with the mask, you can dramatically alter the appearance of the piece (see Figures 1.47 and 1.48).

Figure 1.46 Use Hue/ Saturation set to Colorize to change the hue of the entire brain to a bluish color.

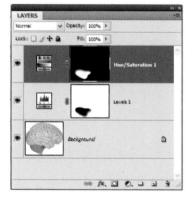

Figure 1.47 Painting may also reveal alterations to areas and leave others alone.

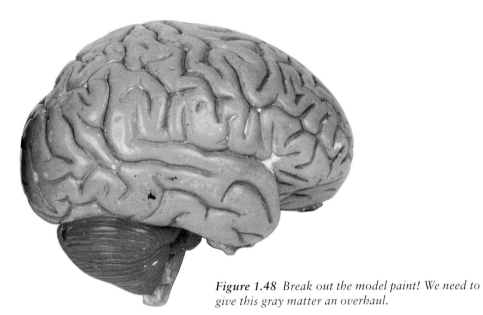

Figure 1.48 Break out the model paint! We need to give this gray matter an overhaul.

Quick Cartoons

You can also add a couple of cartoonish, or "drawn" charac-teristics to the image. Selecting Posterize at the bottom of the Adjustments menu lets you establish the number of levels that appear in the image (see Figure 1.49). This basically separates the image into four levels of color, giving it a drawn or painted quality (see Figure 1.50).

Figure 1.49 A Posterize adjustment layer gives the image a quick "painterly" quality.

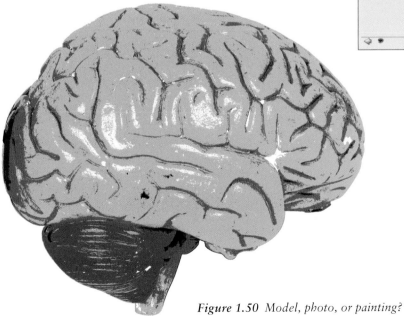

Figure 1.50 Model, photo, or painting?

Keep in mind that all of these adjustments have in no way altered the original photo layer. Simply by adding three adjustment layers, you have been able to enhance the color, repaint an area of the image, and convert it to an artist's rendering. Figure 1.51 shows the Layers panel with all four layers in place.

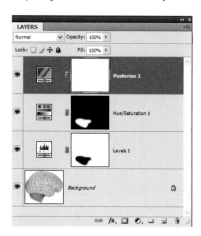

As mentioned in the preceding section, "Working with Layer Masks," you can fade the effects of your adjustments with gray shades, rendering the adjustment semitransparent. Adjustment layers also have to heed the rules of blending modes, so play around a bit and have fun with them. Trust me; you have not seen the last of them in this book!

Figure 1.51 Four layers, three adjustments, and two altered masks give us the final "brain painting."

Displacement Mapping

Have you ever looked at an image created by someone else who seems quite proud of it, but it just doesn't look right to you? You hate to say anything that could be taken as a brutal kick to their ego, but you know deep inside that if they had just taken a few extra steps—a tweak here, an adjustment there—they could have a piece that really boggles the eye. This often occurs when people try to overlay an image on top of another. If the curves and contours of the two images match, the artist is well on the way to creating art that doesn't appear "thrown together."

Displacement maps can help. These are designed to help you conform one image to the shape of another, using the shades of gray in the image to create the distortions in the second. Displacement maps play a part in several of the techniques found later in this book, so a quick hands-on tutorial is in order for you to get up to speed.

Need Direction? Use a Map

Open the images Back.jpg and Map.jpg (see Figure 1.52).

The foundation image for this technique is the photo of a man's back. The thought here is to give him a map tattoo across his shoulders and the back of his head. The second image should work fine, but it first needs to be molded and stretched to match the highlights and shadows on the foundation image.

The best displacement maps tend to be those with the greatest variation in lights and darks. They are created from a channel that you select. Select the Back.jpg image. I've chosen to duplicate the blue channel and use it as the base for my map because it gives the best white-to-black ratio across the image. The highlights are brighter and the shadows are darker than the other channels. Of course, I can tweak these further by using Dodge and Burn, Brightness/Contrast, and so forth, but I prefer to choose the channel that will require a minimal amount of adjusting.

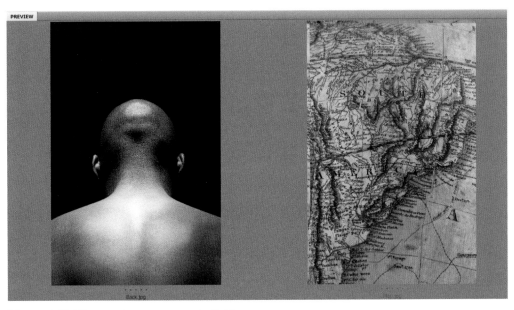

Figure 1.52 *The two images as seen in Bridge*

You can duplicate the blue channel by clicking and dragging it to the Create New Channel icon at the bottom of the Channels panel (second from the right, next to the Trash). A quick Contrast adjustment will help separate the whites and blacks further. I've chosen +25.

Next apply a Gaussian blur to the map channel so that, when it is used to distort the second image, there are no sharp changes and the alterations appear smoother and more transitional (see Figure 1.53).

The last link in the creation of the displacement map is to save it as a new .psd file. To do this, right-click the channel and select Duplicate Channel. In the dialog box that appears, name the new image and be sure to set the Destination setting to New (see Figure 1.54). When the file

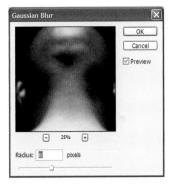

Figure 1.53 *A blur helps conform the image to the map.*

opens as a new image in Photoshop, choose File → Save As and save the new .psd file to your hard disk. Remember where you placed it, because you will need it again shortly. When you have saved the new map, you can close it in Photoshop. Return to the Back.jpg photo and delete the extra channel, as it is no longer needed.

Figure 1.54 *Save the new displacement map as a new document on your hard drive.*

A Peek into a Later Chapter

I'm going to take this opportunity to discuss Apply Image, something I'll cover in depth in Chapter 4, "Texture, Color, and Layer Effects." Apply Image has to be one of my all-time favorite adjustments in Photoshop. I'll reserve most of my praise until later, but because it works for this effect I'll dip into it just a bit here.

Apply Image allows you to blend two images together. Sounds simple enough, until you discover the number of ways you can blend those images. The effects can be rather astounding. For this example, however, all you need to know is that both images must have the exact same dimensions in pixels. I'll discuss why in Chapter 4, but for now simply adjust the size of the Map.jpg image to match the size in pixels of Back.jpg (see Figure 1.55).

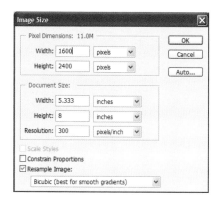

Figure 1.55 *For Apply Image to work, both documents (or all that will be used in creating your final image) need to have the exact same dimensions in pixels.*

You may now use the displacement map to warp the Map.jpg image. Select the map photo and choose Filter → Distort → Displace. The Displace dialog box will then ask you to what Horizontal and Vertical scale you would like the warp to take place. A setting of 10 for each should work fine in this instance, because the images are both 300 ppi. If they were of lower resolution, then lower Scale settings would be in order.

The Displace filter uses a second image (displacement map) to determine how a layer or selection will be distorted.

Also in the Displace dialog box you are asked to choose either Stretch To Fit or Tile. Stretch To Fit works best here, because there is no need to have the edges repeat. For the same reason, Wrap Around should be selected under Undefined Areas (see Figure 1.56). After these settings are selected, click OK to apply the filter.

Figure 1.56 *Setting up the Displace filter*

But wait; there's more! Now Photoshop will ask you what `.psd` image it should use as a map. By default it will take you to the location on your hard disk where you saved the displacement map: simply select it and click OK. The `Map.jpg` image will warp to conform to the contours of the `Back.jpg` photo.

Now on to Apply Image. After you choose Image → Apply Image, you use the Source dropdown list at the top of the dialog box to select the image you would like to apply to your photo. For instance, say you would like a darker, more color-rich version of your current image. You could use Apply Image with the same photo set as the Source, and the Blending mode set to Darken to accomplish this (see Figure 1.57). I've applied the map to the photo of the back (see Figure 1.58).

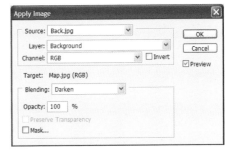

Figure 1.57 Apply Image can use the document you are working on as the Source image.

The combination of displacement maps and Apply Image are only the tip of the iceberg. I'd love to continue this topic now, but I'll force myself to wait until Chapter 4. In the meantime, I have one more cool item to demonstrate in this chapter.

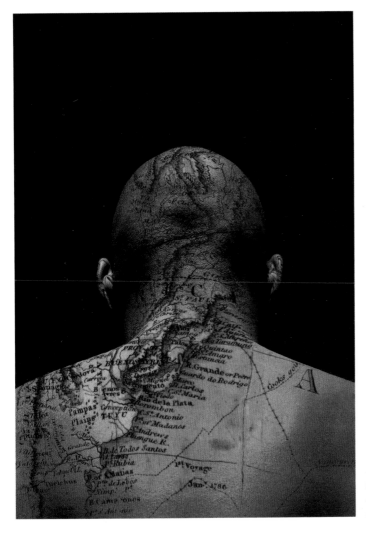

Figure 1.58 Applying an image to itself can have the effect of richer, more vibrant colors.

Discovering the Power of Blend If

My good friend Richard Lynch, whom you may know from his *Hidden Power* books, also published by Sybex, started talking to me about Blend If a few years ago. A typical conversation may have sounded like a Laurel and Hardy routine:

RL: Al, you've got to try Blend If.

AW: Blend what?

RL: Blend If.

AW: Blend if what? What am I blending and why?

RL: Blend If, man! It's the newest thing out there… you're nobody until you get on the Blend If bandwagon!

AW: Dude, I don't know what you're selling, but get it outta here or I'll call the cops. If it's that cool, it can't be legal.

Well, maybe the conversation didn't go exactly like that. But it did pique my interest, especially because his books were the only ones I'd found that even broached the topic. So after much experimenting, head-scratching, and throwing digital paper balls in the cyber-trash, I think (*think*, mind you) that I'm starting to grasp what he's been telling me all these years. At least from a right-brained point of view, I've found a few cool tricks that Blend If can be used for.

Blend If allows you to manipulate how certain colors will react to the color beneath them. Granted, this sounds similar to blending modes, but Blend If is a bit more powerful in that it gives the user control over specific colors in the layer, and not over the entire layer.

For this example, open the image `Wall.jpg`. I've already taken care of generating a displacement map of the wall and applied it to a rasterized type layer. The result is seen in Figure 1.59. Just to prove it to you, Figure 1.60 shows the Layers panel, complete with rasterized text.

Blend If is found in the Blending options of the layer styles, at the top of the left-hand Layer Style dialog box. Not only can you use this cool feature to make the text appear painted onto the wall, but with a little Photoshop magic you can make it appear as though it has aged with the wall, even wiping away those areas of text where the bricks have broken and worn away.

Figure 1.59 Wall photo with a rasterized type layer, pre-distorted with a displacement map

Figure 1.60 The type has already been conformed to the cracks and mortar in the wall image.

To follow along, create a displacement map as we did in the previous tutorial. Generate a text layer, rasterize it, and displace it with the map. Now you are at the point I am with this project.

With the text layer selected, click the FX icon at the bottom of the Layers panel. When the styles menu expands, select Blending Options from the top of the menu. The dialog box in Figure 1.61 appears.

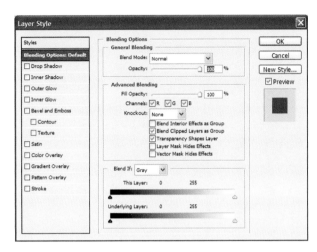

Figure 1.61 *Default Layer Style dialog box with no style settings yet in place*

You need not worry about drop shadows or bevels for this technique. On the lower half of the current window is an area called Advanced Blending. This is where all of the cool Blend If things take place. For instance, I've set Knockout to Shallow. Blend If defaults to gray, so that drop-down can be left alone for now; it is the highlights and shadows I'm concerned with.

At the very bottom is a slider area called Underlying Layer. This means is that if the Wall layer is black, white, or a varying shade of gray, moving the sliders will render portions of the type visible, semitransparent, or invisible. Each slider (right and left) can be split in two by holding down the Option/Alt key and click-sliding it either left or right. This allows you to control the intensity and separation of the blend on your text as it attempts to match the luminosity of the wall. With the sliders in the positions shown in Figure 1.62, the type takes on the faded and aged characteristics shown in Figure 1.63.

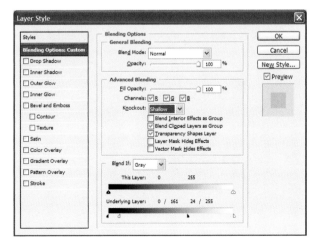

Figure 1.62 *Blend If works on a series of sliders that can be divided to give you more control over the blend.*

Figure 1.63 The text takes on the aged characteristics of the wall beneath.

You can also manipulate the color channels with Blend If. For instance, there is a hint of red in the bricks. You can further age the text by selecting Blend If: Red and adjusting the Underlying Layer sliders as seen in Figure 1.64. Figure 1.65 shows a close-up of the text after this adjustment. You could almost swear that the text was paint that has been around nearly as long as the building, and not simply a type layer altered by Photoshop!

Figure 1.64 Blend If allows you to work with channels to get a more sincere meld between layers.

Figure 1.65 The text looks so real you could swear it has been there for a very long time.

Summary

I've in no way covered every cool tool you will explore in this book on your way to the perfect masterpiece, but I've covered a few of the most important ones, or at least those that will show up frequently. Again, please don't be content to simply use the images supplied with the book.

I encourage you to try these techniques on your own photos, stimulating those right-brain cells and creating your own art. In the next chapter we'll look at editing, correcting, or otherwise altering portraits, so the techniques found in these two chapters should play well together when you sit down with your own photos. I assure you it will be far more gratifying to you, and for me as well, when you have achieved some level of joy when watching your own images come to life using a technique or two you read in these pages.

I can't turn you into an artist, but I suspect there is already one inside you, lurking just beneath the surface and ready to make itself known. If I can help you to realize at least that much by showing you these techniques, then I am indeed a happy man.

So grab your coffee or beverage of choice, grab a digital stack of your own images that could use some sprucing up, and move on to Chapter 2. Get ready... get set...

two

Techniques for Embellishing Portraits

Very few people like the way *they look in photographs. In this chapter you're going to learn how to help with that.*

This chapter deals specifically with the alteration of people—from light portrait retouching to drastic alterations. However, the techniques demonstrated are in no way restricted to images of people; these few examples of corrections and alterations have thousands of possible applications that aren't exclusive to a specific photo type. What the techniques will do is help you work through a process (or at least demonstrate one way of doing things), and after you've learned a procedure, you can then find ideas for applying it to your own artistic renderings. Even better, after the right side of your head is tingling with ideas, you will soon find that you can subtly or drastically alter the steps in a technique to generate some pretty amazing results. Who knows; you could revolutionize a new artistic form—or at least generate some interesting pictures to e-mail to family members.

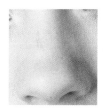

The images referenced as source files for these techniques can be found in the Chapter 2 Source Files folder on this book's CD.

Enhancing Eye Color

I love working with eyes. They've been called windows to the soul, and this is close to the truth. You can discern many things from a person's eyes, from emotional state to truthfulness (or lack thereof). I've known people who swear their eye color changes depending on their mood, and after experiencing a couple of foul tempers, I learned to discern those ill moods just by checking to see whether the eyes were a soothing hazel or a wicked shade of green. Green is rarely good—any fan of comics can tell you that.

Fortunately for me, my love for tweaking eyes works well here, as eye manipulation is a popular topic in the Photoshop community.

The most popular question about working with Photoshop, and therefore the most often answered, is how to solve the red-eye problem. Because that information can be found nearly everywhere, I'm not going to get into it directly; after you are done with this chapter, you will have figured it out; trust me.

What I'll show you first is one way to enhance the existing eye character in a photo. Take a look at Figure 2.1. This is the image eye.jpg from this book's source files; it should be open in Photoshop as you begin. The enhancement you'll add here is to make this mixed color richer and brighter. To do that, you'll use duplicated layers, layer masks, and a couple of blending modes.

Duplicate the Background layer and change the blending mode of the new layer to Overlay. Note that the entire image becomes a bit darker as the new layer blends with the background. This does help enhance the color of the eye, but the skin around the eye becomes darker also. A mask will alleviate this problem quite nicely.

Overlay blending mode either screens or multiplies the pixel information, depending on the base color. Even when colors or patterns overlay pixel information, the highlights and shadows of the original pixels are maintained. The base color is not replaced; rather, it is blended into another form of the original color.

Figure 2.1 *You will enhance the richness of the blue eye color.*

At the bottom of the Layers panel, click the Add Layer Mask icon. By default the mask is filled with white, allowing the contents of the entire layer to be seen. You do not want all of the pixels to be seen, however; just those of the iris and pupil. With the layer mask selected, choose Edit → Fill and fill the mask with black set to 100% opacity and Blending Mode set to Normal. Figure 2.2 shows the Layers panel at this point in the process.

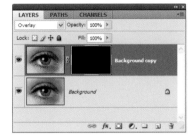

Figure 2.2 *New layer and mask in place*

Set white as the foreground color. Select the Brush tool, and with a soft-edged round brush, paint over the iris and pupil. Adjust the brush size accordingly so that you are painting only within the diameter of the iris. Although it's not necessary to have a steady hand, you may want to create a selection of the area. In this instance the Elliptical Marquee tool will work just fine, because the area being enhanced is round. As you paint, the pixels on this layer will be revealed. The layer is still set to Overlay, so the color of the blended layers comes through (see Figure 2.3).

Figure 2.3 *Painting in the mask*

To brighten the eye a bit (the goal is to brighten the colors without darkening the eye), create a new layer above the Background Copy layer and set the blending mode to Soft Light. With the foreground color still set to white, paint over the iris in this layer also. The change is subtle yet effective. Figures 2.4 and 2.5 show before and after shots. See the difference?

Figure 2.4 *Before lightening*

Figure 2.5 *After lightening*

Altering Eye Color

Altering eye color is simpler than it has ever been, thanks to the Color Replacement tool. This is grouped with the Brush tool and the Pencil tool in the Photoshop CS4 toolbar (Photoshop CS grouped it with the Healing Brush and Patch tools). This powerful and easy-to-use tool relieves a lot of the stress suffered by both amateurs and pros alike, who used to spend a lot of time wishing such a tool existed.

Before I get into the nuts and bolts of this cool feature, let me say that it still has a drawback: it is destructive to the layer (meaning that it alters the pixels), so it is not a miracle cure for every recoloring ailment. In the next variation I'll take you through another process that allows you to preserve the original layer. But first let's do some painting!

Open blue_eyes.jpg (see Figure 2.6) and find the Color Replacement Brush in the toolbar.

Figure 2.6 Window to the mind

As with other tools, this one has settings that can be changed on the Options bar. For this technique, set the blending mode to Hue and ensure that Find Edges is selected for the Limits setting. Brush Diameter should be 20, Sampling Mode should be Continuous, Tolerance should be 30%, and Anti-alias should be checked. With the Find Edges setting, Photoshop will look for boundaries to paint within while the new color is being applied, thus allowing only the hue of the iris and not the areas outside it to change.

Hue blending mode creates a color based on the luminance and saturation of the base color and hue/tone of the blend color.

Before you change the color of the eyes, you will want to choose a new color. Open the Color Picker (click the foreground color) and select a new color (see Figure 2.7). Click OK.

Duplicate the Background layer to keep the original image unaltered and start painting over the iris with an appropriately sized brush. I love the Hue setting, because the color change is subtle yet clearly evident (see Figure 2.8). The reflections are retained, the pupil remains black, and the eye color still looks natural.

For colors that are richer, change the blending mode of the brush to Saturation. A richer green is displayed, but the eye clearly looks manipulated and unnatural (see Figure 2.9).

This can be quickly adjusted by lowering the Opacity setting of the top layer to 10–20%, giving a far more natural appearance.

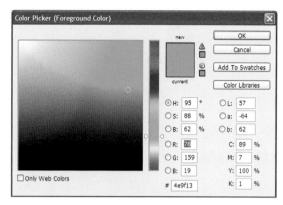

Figure 2.7 Choose the new eye color.

Delete the previously retouched layer and duplicate the Background layer. Change the blending mode of the brush to Color. Those of you familiar with retouching may recognize this mode, because it was a primary mode for retouching in earlier versions of Photoshop.

Paint over the iris again. If the color is still too outlandish, reduce the layer opacity to 30–40%. When I'm working with eyes and lips, the Color blending mode is by far my favorite. The eye color teeters on the edge of natural and unnatural; it could be real, but it could be enhanced—at least that is what viewers will think, and I like to keep them guessing (see Figure 2.10).

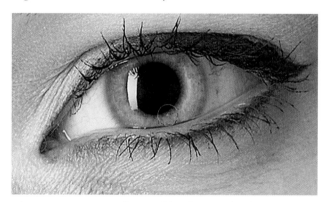

Figure 2.8 By using the Hue blending mode, the changed color in this example retains a natural appearance.

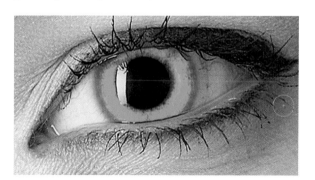

Figure 2.9 Replacing the color in Saturation mode gives this image a much more artificial appearance.

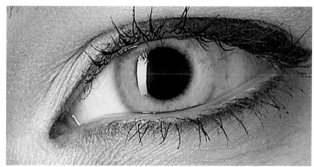

Figure 2.10 Enhancing eye color with the Color blending mode

If the brush ignored your command telling it to stay within the borders of the iris, a layer mask can fix the problem. Just create a mask for the layer and paint with black over the color that extends beyond the iris. Another alternative to correcting spot areas is the

History Brush. When finished, your model should have a new set of peepers, or at least colored contact lenses (see Figure 2.11).

Figure 2.11 Creating eyes of green

Color blending mode creates a color based on the luminance of the base color, hue, and saturation of the blend color.

Altering Hair Color

To demonstrate that similar processes have multiple applications and that you shouldn't make things harder than they have to be, let's apply a similar coloring technique to altering hair color.

Open the image punk.jpg (see Figure 2.12). Note that this photo has already had some exposure and color manipulation applied to it. I've chosen this image to demonstrate that even manipulated photos can be altered to meet an artist's or photographer's requirements.

Duplicate the Background layer and select the Brush tool. Set the blending mode for the brush to Color and set the other options as shown here:

Brush	90
Opacity	30%
Flow	50%

Select a color and place it in the foreground. Use the brush to paint over the hair sweeping off to the side and follow the hairline. Continue painting until all the red pixels have been swapped with the new color (see Figure 2.13).

Figure 2.12 *Red-haired model*

Figure 2.13 *Changing the red to purple*

I bet you guessed how to clean up the excess paint that has spilled over. If you said layer mask or History Brush, you are absolutely right! See how things work together for the common good?

For a little added splash, create a new layer above the painted layer and set the blending mode for the new layer to Color (see Figure 2.14). Select varying shades of color for the foreground (green, blue, mauve, stucco…) and paint over a few strands of hair. Use Figure 2.15 as a reference if you like.

Figure 2.14 *New layer set to Color blending mode*

Figure 2.15 *Trying out a variety of colors*

Variation: Subtly Enhancing Highlights and Natural Hair Color

The previous technique showed a pretty drastic alteration, but the majority of alterations that people attempt in Photoshop are subtle—simply enhancing color or changing it slightly. Here's one method for changing color that retains the natural look of the hair.

Open the image `retouch.jpg` (see Figure 2.16).

You will start by adding highlights, so duplicate the Background layer. Select the Dodge tool and change the options to these:

Brush	80
Range	Midtones
Exposure	35%

Figure 2.16 Our hair model

Using the Dodge tool, brighten a few strands of hair similar to the painting of color done in the previous technique. Do not dodge the hair too much; a few highlighted strands will do (see Figure 2.17).

Figure 2.17 Highlights with Dodge

Next you can add color as in the previous technique, but drastically toned down. Create a new layer and set the blending mode to Color. Select a color somewhere between red, orange, and brown as the foreground color and paint over the hair in the new layer (see Figure 2.18). The adjusted image is shown in Figure 2.19. If the color is too harsh for your taste or needs, simply lower the opacity of the painted layer.

Figure 2.18 New layer in Color mode... again

Figure 2.19 The finished result

Enhancing Lip Color

In a manner similar to the eye technique covered earlier, lips can also be enhanced and given new life digitally. This technique is especially popular for women—they can now look as though they spent hours meticulously applying makeup without even cracking the seal on their lipstick.

One idea I want to work into your way of thinking (if it's not already there) is that techniques you've seen performed on eyes, hair, leaves, concrete, or whatever can also be used to enhance other texture types, other subjects, and so forth. Although both eyes and lips reside in the same neighborhood on a body, the characteristics that make eyes recognizable as eyes and lips as lips are very different. But just because the color and texture are different does not mean that similar techniques to color or correct them cannot be used.

Open the image `grin.tif` (see Figure 2.20). The woman in this photo doesn't really need a lot of makeup, but her lips could be a bit richer in tone. This technique will use the colors already resident in the image as the foundation palette.

As before, create a duplicate of the Background layer and set the blending mode to Overlay. Because the lips are the target of this piece, notice how they take on a deeper shade of red.

To deepen the hue even further, select the Burn tool and set the Brush to 70, the Range to Midtones, and the Exposure to 50%. Before you darken things too much, keep in mind that not all people require multiple applications of makeup. You may wish to try the next step with a reduced exposure setting. Again, experimentation is encouraged.

Run the brush over the lips, being careful not to linger too long in the same place or to burn the same area repeatedly. If you do linger or make multiple passes, the Burn tool will continue to saturate the pixels until they become extremely dark. In nice, easy strokes, run the brush over the lips until the richer reds emerge. If you overdo it with this tool, the lips will gradually turn black, so take it easy!

Figure 2.20 *What could she be thinking?*

The Burn tool has its foundation in traditional photography. Burning is used in that medium to increase exposure to areas of a print, and the Burn tool in Photoshop works in the same manner. You can use it to increase saturation in a photo, darkening select areas.

Create a mask for this layer and fill it with black. In the mask, paint with white over the lips to reveal the richer tones (see Figure 2.21).

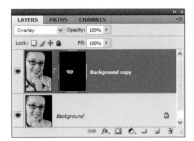

Figure 2.21 Black hides, white reveals.

Figure 2.22 shows the final corrected image with just these simple adjustments. The new lips appear to have a light application of makeup, without being over-the-top. Sometimes it's cool to be subtle.

Figure 2.22 Pale to deep red in a couple of quick steps

Whitening Teeth

Photoshop can help you put a sparkle on those pearly whites in no time.

Open say_cheese.jpg. Figure 2.23 shows the teeth you will be working on for this technique. I chose this image because I hate having my real teeth cleaned and because the teeth themselves (the photo's teeth, not mine) are tinted yellow as the result of age.

Duplicate the Background layer and lighten the teeth with the Dodge tool. You need not take out all the yellow—just lighten the teeth a bit.

Next, create a new layer and change the blending mode to Saturation. Select a light-gray foreground color, and with the Brush tool, paint over the teeth in the new layer. You can also accomplish this by choosing white but reducing the opacity of the paint. You will notice the yellow hue disappear as if by magic (or at least a powerful toothpaste). See Figure 2.24.

> Saturation blending mode creates a color based on the luminance and hue of the base color and saturation of the blend color. Gray produces no change, because there is no saturation associated with gray.

You can whiten the teeth by changing the blending mode of the brush to Hue, with these settings:

Brush	100
Opacity	45%
Flow	75%

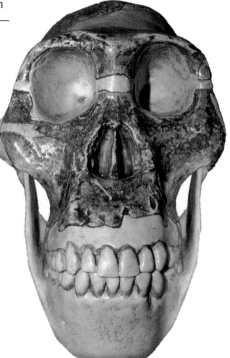

Figure 2.23 *Yellow smile?*

If you want to make the teeth look like they have been over-bleached, simply select the Background Copy layer again and apply the Dodge tool to all the canines, molars, and bicuspids you want until the smile meets with your satisfaction (see Figure 2.25).

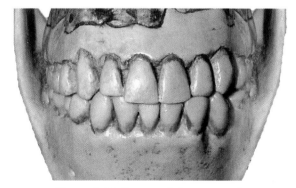

Figure 2.24 *Some staining removed*

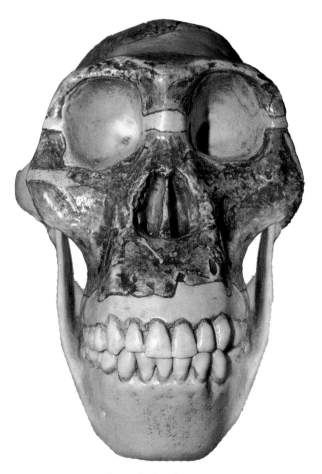

Figure 2.25 A smile made for the movies and politics

Removing Acne and Blemishes

Let's take a break from painting, dodging, and burning, and tackle another issue that appeals to retouchers everywhere. When I was going through those wonderful transition years from boy to grown-up, I suffered from a rather active case of acne. I absolutely hated it, and because Photoshop did not yet exist, I had to suffer through far too many photo sessions without any chance of the retouching that kids today have available. Having pictures taken for the yearbook was bad enough, but when you became a senior, the pictures were printed in... egad... full color!

That particular problem has thankfully faded into the distant past, but a couple of scars remain—both on my face and on my psyche. As with teeth and hair, Photoshop can act as a digital cosmetic surgeon with just a few quick tool applications.

Have the image candid_glance.jpg ready in Photoshop. As you can see in Figure 2.26, this lovely young woman has a few minor blemishes apparent on her cheeks, which don't look bad at normal resolution. When you zoom in (see Figure 2.27), blackheads and old acne scars become painfully apparent because of the high resolution of this image. If this shot were part of a model's portfolio, who knows what jobs she might lose?

Figure 2.26 In a normal view, the model's old acne scars are barely visible. But zoom in, and...

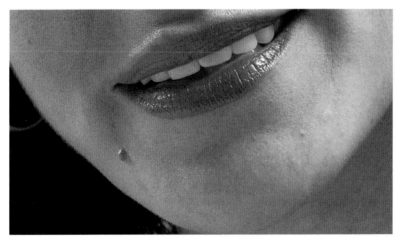

Figure 2.27 ...Toooo much detail!

Cleaning up the scars is simply a matter of covering them with samples taken from areas of the face without blemishes. Select the Spot Healing Brush tool and enter these settings in the Options bar:

Brush	25
Mode	Normal
Type	Proximity Match

Move the cursor over an offending spot and simply click with the mouse. That blemish is quickly replaced with a smooth sample taken from regions around the area being corrected. For instance, the mole on her chin is wiped away with one click, replacing the area with smooth skin (see Figure 2.28).

Figure 2.28 *New skin stamped into place*

Although they are separate tools, the Clone Stamp tool and the Healing Brush tool often work best in conjunction with each other. Select the Healing Brush tool and enter these settings in the Options bar:

Brush	30
Mode	Normal
Source	Sampled

Again, sample a clear area of skin near where the blemishes were covered, and release the Option/Alt key. Apply the sample to the areas of discoloration (see Figure 2.29).

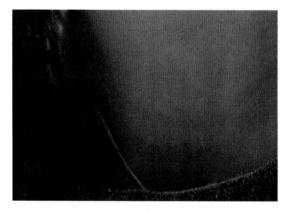

Figure 2.29 *Moles and color replaced with new skin*

Figures 2.30 and 2.31 show an area of scarring between the model's eyebrows that is easily corrected by using the same technique.

Just a few simple corrections (Figure 2.32) and this model is ready to work.

Figure 2.30
Acne scar

Figure 2.31 Skin smooth
once again

Figure 2.32 Picture of health

Erasing Wrinkles

This technique is also one close to my heart, and it gets cozier there with each passing day. Having officially surpassed that cumbersome middle-aged mark, I trust that I'll be looking for even more ways to imitate Dorian Gray (or at least in reverse, if that makes sense).

Take a look at Figure 2.33 (sigh.jpg). This lady looks to be aging gracefully, but doesn't look too happy about it nonetheless.

I'm sure you can help her out, though, and the process is very simple.

Duplicate the Background layer. By using the Clone Stamp tool, the Spot Healing Brush, or the Healing Brush tool (any of the three works just fine), sample clear unwrinkled areas of the skin and then apply them to the wrinkles. Don't worry if she takes on an unnatural, baby-smooth appearance, as in Figure 2.34. To finish this correction, simply lower the opacity of the Background Copy layer until some of the wrinkles beneath show through (see Figure 2.35).

Figure 2.33 Smile, and the laugh lines smile with you.

Figure 2.34 Stamp the new skin over the wrinkles.

Figure 2.35 She looks 10 years younger!

Digital Liposuction

This technique uses the image tummy-2.jpg. Please open it now.

Notoriously, the camera adds 10 pounds. And even though most people who enjoy that sort of thing would not pay to see someone too thin belly dancing, the model for this technique (see Figure 2.36) has decided that her publicity stills should look a little skinnier than she actually is. In particular, she doesn't like the love handles in her photos. Whether she needs slimming or not, the Photoshop physician can help.

One way to trim down the love handles and still keep a natural curve is to generate a path and trim away the excess. Select the Pen tool and, in the Options bar, click the Paths button in the upper left. Select the standard Pen tool (as opposed to the Freeform Pen tool) Check out the options for the tool in Figure 2.37.

Figure 2.36 I dream of Jeannie.

Figure 2.37 Pen tool options

This tool can be tricky and is pretty daunting to those who don't use it on a regular basis. It isn't that difficult to work with after you play with it a bit, though.

Take a look at Figure 2.38. First, click the mouse just above where you want the correction to be made. Click another point along the seam of her pantaloons and, holding down the mouse button, drag to the left so that the adjustment handles appear. Then just manipulate the mouse until you get the curve you want.

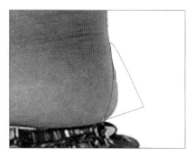

Figure 2.38 Create a path around the love handle.

To help you generate perfect curves when using the Pen tool, practice dragging the first adjustment handle in the direction the bump of the curve is to go, and the second adjustment handle in the opposite direction. This formula will create an S curve. For more information on Curves, consult "Drawing with the Pen Tool" in the Adobe Photoshop CS4 Help Files.

Click in the white area to create a new point, and then click on the first point to close the path. By closing the path, I mean that all the points of the path will be connected so that a "circle" is formed. At the bottom of the Paths panel, click the Load Path As Selection icon. This will create an active selection following the path (see Figure 2.39).

This edit is fairly simple, because the subject is already on a white background. To trim away the love handle, just create a new layer at the top of the layer stack and fill it with white (see Figure 2.40). If the subject were on a different background, you would need additional steps (extracting and deleting the excess pixels) to complete the retouching.

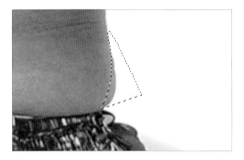
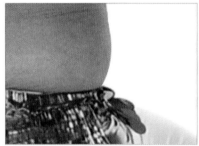
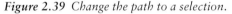

Figure 2.39 *Change the path to a selection.*   ***Figure 2.40*** *Fill the selection with white to wipe away a couple of pounds.*

Variation: Using the Liquify Filter

Another way to tighten up those elusive curves is to use the Pucker tool in the Liquify Filter dialog box. Use the same image as before (tummy-2.jpg); either open a new instance of it or click the original state in the History panel to revert to the unaltered photo.

The Pucker tool, found in the Liquify Filter dialog box, moves the pixels within the brush area toward the center of the brush while you either hold down the mouse button or drag. The longer this tool is applied, the more compressed the pixels in the brush area will appear.

Choose Filter → Liquify. Select the Pucker tool on the left, and then set up these options/settings for the tool on the right-hand side:

Brush Size   35
Brush Density   60
Brush Rate   80

You are reducing the brush size and density from their default of 100, because the pinching of pixels that occurs when using this tool needs to be gradual. This simply gives you better control and will help prevent harsh distortions. The Liquify tool likes to manhandle pixels, and overapplication will quickly stretch and pull the image to the point where the subject is no longer recognizable as a life form.

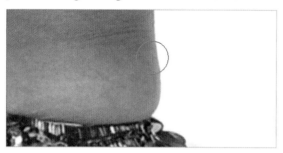

Figure 2.41 Reduce the love handles again—gently!

Now center the cursor over the inside edge of the skin of the love handle. As you click and hold the left mouse button, the pixels surrounding the cursor will be drawn toward its center. Slowly move the mouse up and down the edge, to the seam of the pantaloons, and watch how the pixels are drawn in. *Do not* linger in one spot for long, or the edge will become lumpy and distorted (see Figure 2.41).

Another place where women (and some men) want to look more like a fashion model than a belly dancer is the upper arms (see Figure 2.42). Using the same careful technique, pull the fat in on this area also.

Figure 2.42 Shrink the fat forming on the upper arms in the same way.

After you have the hang of the process, reduce the exposed shoulder, forearm, and the other side of her waist to keep her body in proportion (see Figure 2.43). That is the main problem (and a major attraction for a lot of users) with overapplication of this filter: the loss of believable proportions. Using it delicately, however, can create some startlingly realistic results, as you will see later in the book.

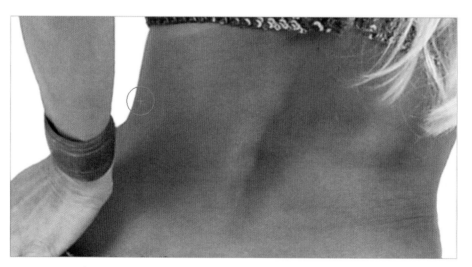

Figure 2.43 Slimming

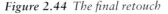

Figure 2.44 *The final retouch*

Now that the model has been trimmed and tucked in her upper areas, we've left her with a rather prominent backside. You don't think so? Trust me, if she stood up right now she would be asking for—rather, *demanding*—her money back.

To fix this, increase the size of the brush and run it over her derriere until the proportions look right to you. Figure 2.44 shows the final shot; another proud customer of the Photoshop Weight Loss Program.

Digital Face-Lift

This technique uses the image `facelift.jpg`. Please open the photo now.

I've already touched on wrinkle reduction in this chapter, but the changes made there were fairly subtle, more to enhance the photograph rather than the subject of the photo. That was a studio technique a customer might find flattering. This technique takes the process of wrinkle reduction to the extreme, by physically altering the image of the subject to reduce age and give the appearance that she really isn't in her early 60s but ceased aging years earlier.

When I first started playing with digital face-lifts, my subjects often ended up looking like some creature that could survive only in the imagination. After numerous failed attempts, I began looking at how real cosmetic surgeons approached their work and altered their clients. Most of the changes a person undergoes are subtle: a slight narrowing of the bridge of the nose, a removal of skin so that the remaining skin can be pulled back to remove wrinkles, and so forth. If the client elects for more trips to the surgeon, the alterations become increasingly apparent until the skin appears stretched, the lips cease moving in a natural way, and the eyes seem in a permanently open state. I won't name any names, but I'll bet you can pinpoint some examples of cosmetic-surgery extremes.

Just because it can be done in Photoshop does not mean that a plastic surgeon could get the same results! Playing with pixels is one thing, but my publisher and I accept no liability for what might happen if you alter your picture and then ask a surgeon to duplicate the effect. You're beautiful just the way you are; having known you for two chapters now, I wouldn't change a thing.

On to the technique. The woman in Figure 2.45 has wonderful skin tone and bone structure, but the years have added a few creases and an age mark or two that can certainly be wiped away digitally. The primary correction in this photo will be wrinkle reduction as performed earlier in the book, but this will be combined with a few other adjustments to create a younger-looking, albeit still mature, businesswoman.

Figure 2.45 *Our subject, before digital cosmetic surgery*

Start by duplicating the Background layer. The woman has many fine wrinkles all over her face and neck, but her cheek (see Figure 2.46) has a smooth area that can be used to clean up the rest of her face. Select the Healing Brush tool and, with the following options, take a sample of the smooth skin:

Brush	50–80
Mode	Normal
Source	Sampled

Although similar to the Clone Stamp tool, the Healing Brush not only applies a sample (or pattern) to an area, but also attempts to match the texture, shading, lighting, and transparency of the pixels it is applied to (source pixels). The result gives far better seamless blending than the Clone Stamp in the case of facial reconstruction and other effects.

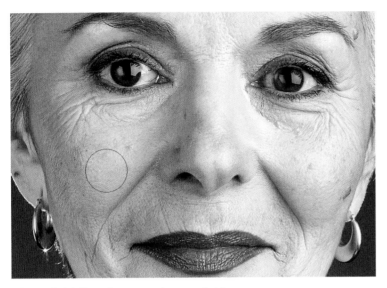

Figure 2.46 *Sample a smooth area of skin.*

Apply the sample beneath the woman's eye and on her lid to clean up the minute folds and discoloration seen there. Overlay most of the wrinkles seen in this portion of the face, but leave a couple of tiny crow's-feet. Repeat the process around her other eye and also take out the more prominent wrinkles on her forehead (see Figure 2.47).

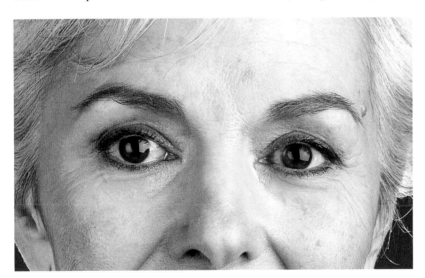

Figure 2.47 *Age around the eyes reduced*

Move down to the lower portion of her face, as well as her neck (see Figure 2.48). To correct this area, take another sample from the smooth area on her chin to cover the mole that is being carefully, but not entirely successfully, concealed by makeup. This technique is the same as the touch-up done on the young woman earlier in this chapter (removing acne and blemishes), although the wrinkles here are more pronounced and frequent. A few wrinkles are needed for realism, but most can go away (see Figure 2.49).

Figure 2.48 *Chin and cheeks, pre-alteration*

Figure 2.49 *Chin and cheeks after new skin is applied*

Continue the same technique on her neck. Take samples of the smooth areas on her neck and apply the Healing Brush tool in the same manner as before, covering the lines that years of head turning have produced.

You will now get a bit more practice with Liquify. The Liquify tool is fantastic for digital face-lifting, as long as it isn't overdone. You will use it to tighten the areas of the face that have been pulled and stretched by gravity. This is going to help shave years off the woman.

Choose Filter → Liquify. As in the previous technique, the size of the Pucker brush (no larger than needed to make small corrections), reduced density, and reduced pressure will help draw in the flabby skin. These are the settings that I've found work the best:

Brush Size	50–80
Brush Density	40–60
Brush Pressure	40–60
Brush Rate	50–80

Look at Figure 2.50, which shows the woman before any Liquify adjustments. What you want to do here is run the tool along the cheeks, much as you would if using the Highlighter during an extraction. Do not linger in one place for long; move the mouse as fluidly as possible (see Figure 2.51). Reduce the nose size, and pucker the areas above and below her eyes to open them a bit (see Figure 2.52). Also, move along the edges of her neck to slim it.

After you have finished Liquifying, you can employ the hair-coloring techniques described earlier in this chapter. Note that proceeding with hair coloring will most likely make the image retouching look obvious, so if you want a natural feel to the end result, I'd forgo treating the hair. I'll proceed with hair treatments here but thought you should be aware of the downside.

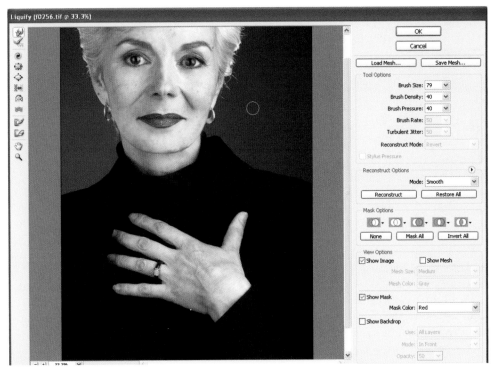

Figure 2.50 *It's time to reduce the effects of time.*

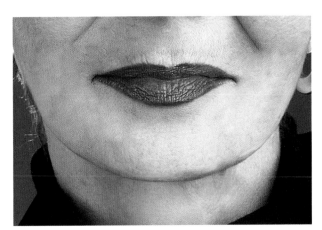

Figure 2.51 *Rounding the chin has a staggering effect on the aging process.*

Figure 2.52 *Lifting the eyes and narrowing the nose also helps restore some lost vigor.*

As a refresher, I'll step through the process quickly:

1. Select a color for the woman's hair and place it in the foreground. Create a new layer.
2. Change the blending mode of the new layer to Color and, with the Paintbrush tool set to Soft Light, paint over the woman's hair in the new layer. If the color is a bit stark for your tastes, try reducing the opacity of the paint layer or changing the blending mode to Soft Light (Figures 2.53 and 2.54).

Figure 2.53 *New layer for hair coloring*

Figure 2.54 *Blending mode of the brush set to Soft Light for a more natural look*

When finished, you will have a much younger-looking version of the original woman. I hope that you have a greater appreciation for the Liquify filter than when you started. It is a great tool for massive distortions of features but is also powerful and masterful at slight alterations. Often the slightest changes can make all the difference in the world (see Figures 2.55 and 2.56). You may want to lower the layer opacity so you can better blend the effects with the original layer.

Figure 2.55 *One more look at the model before her digital makeover*

Figure 2.56 *From mid 60s to late 40s, thanks to Photoshop*

Summary

Corrections, manipulations, alterations…with the technology available to home users, let alone digital editing professionals, it truly is hard to discern the 'real' from the 'enhanced'. As you have seen in this chapter, this is particularly true where portraits are concerned. The next chapter steers away from the not-so-obvious manipulations and focuses on the obvious. Let's take a peak at the party going on in the right half of the skull and get a little groovy, shall we?

three

A Few Right-Brained Special Effects

One of the side benefits *of being an author of Photoshop books and articles is being asked to teach the software in a classroom. As I go through the course, eventually I get to the Liquify Filter. As soon as I mention we will be working with that feature, the mood of the class always changes from attentive study to giddy expectation: they know we are about to do something "cool." I bet I could create an entire month's worth of curricula and fill every seat in the room simply by warping faces. People like Practical, but people love Cool.*

This chapter is not about the Liquify Filter, but rather about using images to build ideas. I'll introduce a few special effects designed to expand your understanding of what the software is capable of and to add a few nifty tricks to your digital arsenal. Photographs will be used, but they serve as foundations for the end effect rather than the end product itself. Continue reading, and I'll demonstrate what I mean.

The images referenced as source files for these techniques can be found in the Chapter 3 Source Files *folder on this book's CD.*

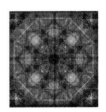

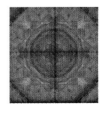

Creating a Glass Sphere

An effect does not have to be difficult or the process exceptionally long to give it the *special* moniker. Case in point: glass-sphere effects have been around since Photoshop's humble beginnings. This is one of those effects that can be created in a myriad of ways with multiple variations. The end result can be simplistic or complex, depending on how much time the artist puts into the project. The more time spent working on the sphere, the more realistic (one hopes) the glass is going to be.

Here, you're going to take an image and apply a sphere effect to it.

Forming the Sphere

 Open the image fish.jpg on the book's CD (see Figure 3.1). I believe you'll find that the colors inherent in a photo add to the end effect in many cases, and the glass-sphere technique definitely benefits from the colors in the photograph itself.

Figure 3.1 *The colors in this photo will add character to the glass sphere in the end piece.*

By now you should be in the habit of duplicating the Background layer at the beginning of these projects, so duplicate the Background layer now. Rename the new layer **Sphere** (see Figure 3.2).

Before proceeding, stop and think about glass for a moment. We are all familiar with what a marble looks like, and in particular a semitransparent marble. What characteristics do you envision in your mind's eye that define this object as a marble? For one, a marble is round. That's a good starting point. In the case of a glass, semitransparent marble, you might note that objects behind the marble

Figure 3.2 *Duplicate the Background layer and call the new layer Sphere.*

are distorted when seen through the glass; what you see will appear curved to match the shape of the glass. Another characteristic is how light plays on the surface and in the interior of the sphere. You'll have reflections and assorted bright spots, as well as darker areas caused by the density of the glass around the curves.

With these points in mind, you can take your Photoshop knowledge and attempt to duplicate on the monitor what you see in your mind. Using the Sphere layer as a foundation, you will see in a few short steps the central portion of the image magnified through a reflective glass spherical object.

You'll start by making a spherical selection on the Sphere layer. To create a perfectly round selection, the Elliptical Marquee tool is the tool of choice. Certainly you could draw a selection freehand to try to create a perfect circle, but that's not necessary. On the Options bar, you'll see several options available for the Elliptical Marquee tool when it is selected in the toolbar. One of these settings that can be changed is a drop-down menu labeled Style. The default setting is Normal, which will allow you to draw the ratio and size of the selection freehand. Expanding this menu, you'll see a selection called Fixed Ratio. Selecting this allows you to draw a perfect circle every time. The tool's settings for this example are as follows:

Selection Type	New Selection
	(New Selection button pressed on the Options bar)
Feather	0
Anti-alias	Checked
Style	Fixed Ratio
Width	1
Height	1

You can now draw your circle selection. Start in the upper-left corner, maybe an inch or two vertically and horizontally from the corner of the photo. Continue drawing your selection to the lower right so that the fish's head is entirely encompassed by the selection. Figure 3.3 shows what the selection should look like when you're done.

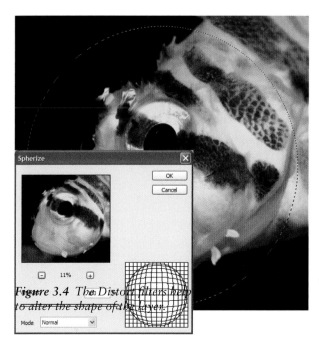

Figure 3.4 The Distort filters help to alter the shape of the layer.

Figure 3.3 Make a circular selection around the fish's head.

With the selection active, you're ready to start creating the sphere. The first step is to apply the Spherize filter to the selection. Choose Filter → Distort → Spherize. The Spherize dialog box that appears allows you to tell Photoshop that you'd like to conform a selection or layer to a sphere. The setting of choice here is Normal mode, which comes up by default. Set the amount of the distortion to 100%. You can decrease the Zoom in the viewer window to better see how the filter will affect your selection. Click OK to accept the change (see Figure 3.4).

To ensure we are working simply on the sphere, keep the selection active and go to Layer → New → Layer Via Copy. ⌘/Ctrl-click the new layer to activate the selection again.

Enhancing with Light and Shadows

There are more filters you can use to get closer to a glass effect. The Lens Flare filter is perfect for generating reflections that appear on the glass and are refracted through it. With the

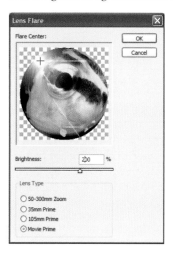

Figure 3.5 *Lens Flare allows you to select a lens type and position angle. How light plays on this image will determine how realistic the final sphere appears.*

selection still active, choose Filter → Render → Lens Flare. When the Lens Flare dialog box appears, you'll notice you have four Lens Type choices. Select Movie Prime and set the Brightness level slider to 200%. You may click on the crosshairs in the example window and move it manually. The location of the crosshairs in the example window indicates where the light hits the surface of the sphere. Move it to the upper-left quadrant of the glass (see Figure 3.5).

Using some variety in reflection types sometimes helps with the realism of the final project, so apply the Lens Flare filter once more, only this time select 35mm Prime as the Lens Type. Move the Brightness slider to about 130%. This will reduce the amount of glare. Also reposition the crosshairs to the lower-right corner of the glass (see Figure 3.6). This will be the exit point of the light through the semitransparent sphere.

After you have the second Lens Flare in position, click OK to accept the settings. Now you can move on and manually add to the reflections in the glass, as well as darken areas that will help add to the realism. Dodge and Burn will perform these functions to perfection.

Click the Dodge tool in the toolbar. Note that the Options bar changes to reflect the settings you can apply to this tool. First choose a 200-pixel Soft Round brush. Set the Range of the brush to Highlights. When you apply the tool to light areas in the layer, they will gradually increase in brightness. If you continue to use the Dodge tool in an area, the area will gradually become stark white. Set the Exposure to 70% (see Figure 3.7).

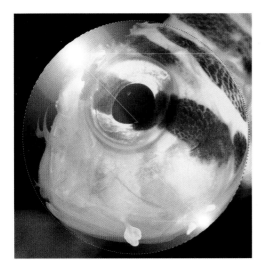

Figure 3.6 *An additional Lens Flare application lets you determine an exit point of the light passing through the glass object.*

Figure 3.7 *The Dodge tool options*

Apply the Dodge tool just as if you were painting with the Paintbrush. Run the Dodge tool over the bright area where light hits the glass in the upper-left corner. The more you apply the tool, the brighter this area will become. Also work the tool in the lower-right area, although not as much as you did in the upper left. If you look at Figure 3.8, you'll see that I've also applied the Dodge tool to a spot in the center of the selection and to a few light areas around the perimeter of the selection. Again, think of how light plays on and through that imaginary marble.

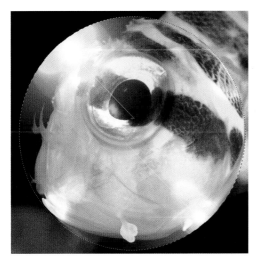

Figure 3.8 *Applying Dodge to lit points on the sphere enhances the effects applied with the Lens Flare filter.*

The Burn tool is applied in the same manner as Dodge. Select the Burn tool and, in the Options bar, set the Range to Midtones (see Figure 3.9). This will help darken the colored areas of the selection, especially along the edges of the sphere. Why is this important?

Primarily it helps to distinguish the edge along the curve of the surface from the background (the unaltered portions of the layer). Figure 3.10 demonstrates the effect.

Figure 3.9 The Burn tool options

Figure 3.10 Darkening the edges helps to define where the glass begins, separating it from the background.

Including Imperfections

After the Burn tool has been applied, the glass is basically complete. You can add additional glasslike imperfections to the sphere if you like. One such blemish occurs when the glass is blown improperly and bubbles form in the interior. If you were to look at these imperfections closely, you would most likely see a smaller version of the scenery behind the sphere.

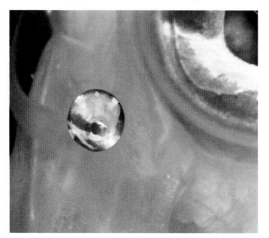

By copying the sphere you just created, placing it on a new layer, and shrinking it with the Transform tools, you can come close to duplicating this effect. Play with the blending modes of the layer for added flavor. In Figure 3.11 I've made a copy of the sphere, transformed the size and aspect, and changed the blending mode for the new mini-sphere to Overlay.

Let's see what has been achieved. Figure 3.12 is the final glass sphere, complete with distortions, reflections, shadows, and refractions.

Figure 3.11 Adding imperfections to the glass is a stylish touch.

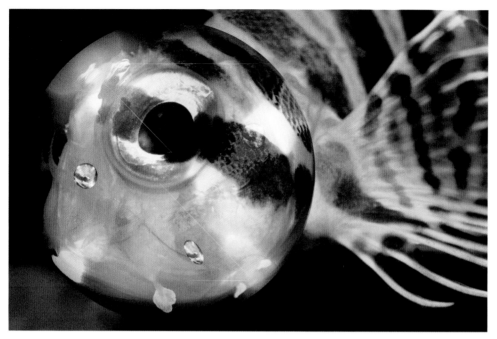

Figure 3.12 The final image. The fish eye is magnified through a sphere of glass.

The technique I've demonstrated is not simply restricted to glass. You could use these same steps (or variations thereof) to create bubbles, electrified crystal balls, and other semi-transparent globes. What you hope to see in the depths of the sphere is up to you.

Intertwining Objects

Masking is a wonderful tool for blending layers or making selective alterations and corrections. These types of edits are fairly standard—and expected. For a person of a creative persuasion, they might be a bit mundane. This is a book for creative types, so standard uses simply won't do in every instance. I look at the masking features and say "What else can I make this do?"

My thoughts then turn away from blending layers, and toward tying or intertwining objects in layers together. Something like a Celtic knot, but with real-world objects. Open the image fork.tif (see Figure 3.13). Let's see if we can tie these tines together, or at least give the appearance of such.

In Chapter 1 we extracted an apple from its background using the Path tool. I'm not going to walk through the process again, but I want you to perform the same function on the fork by creating a path around the handle and tines to prepare the fork for extraction. Once the path is complete and closed, the Paths panel should like Figure 3.14.

Once the path has been created, click on the Load Path As Selection icon on the bottom of the Paths panel. Copy the selection (⌘/Ctrl+C) and paste the fork into a new blank layer (⌘/Ctrl+V). Turn off the Background layer (see Figure 3.15).

Figure 3.13 Get ready to dig into layer masks.

Figure 3.14 Create a path around the fork to prepare it for extraction.

Figure 3.15 Create a new layer to house the fork.

Before we begin twisting the tines together, there are some color issues to take care of as a few stray pixels along the edges of the object most likely still retain the background color. For this example, we will remove the color by generating a selection around the fork in the extracted layer. Change the foreground color to Black and select the Paintbrush. On the Options bar set Opacity to 100%, Flow to 100%, and Blending to Hue. Paint along the edges of the selection to remove the red/orange tint that may remain and replace it with a steel gray (see Figure 3.16).

Rotate the image 90 degrees clockwise (Image → Image Rotation → 90° CW). Reposition the extracted fork to the right side of the canvas with the Move tool or arrow keys. If you use the arrow keys, hold down the Shift key at the same time to speed up the process. You'll want to center the tines in the document to allow room for the technique. Duplicate the fork layer you rotated earlier and flip the new copy horizontally (Edit → Transform → Flip Horizontal). Reposition the new layer on the left side of the document so the tines of both forks overlap in the middle of the image (see Figure 3.17).

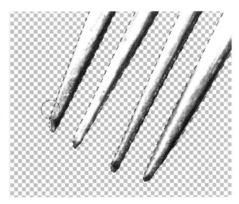

Figure 3.16 *Using the Hue blending mode for the Paintbrush wipes away offending colors.*

Figure 3.17 *Prepare the layers for intertwining.*

Create a layer mask for the topmost fork layer. By default the mask will be filled with white, revealing the contents of the layer. What we want to do now is create areas of black in the mask that will hide alternating sections of the tines, giving the image an interlocked appearance.

⌘/Ctrl-click the bottom *visible* fork layer, but ensure the mask for the top layer is selected. Fill the resulting selection in the mask with Black (see Figure 3.18).

Press the D key to ensure the foreground color is white (the default when the mask is selected). Select the Brush tool and choose a brush slightly larger than the thickness of the tines. Paint over alternating sections of the tines *in the mask*, revealing the topmost layer in those areas once again (see Figure 3.19).

The result will leave the tines interwoven together, as you can see in Figure 3.20.

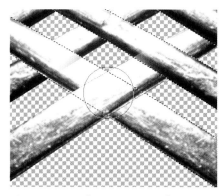

Figure 3.18 *Fill the selection in the mask with Black.*

Figure 3.19 *White paint reveals portions of the tines.*

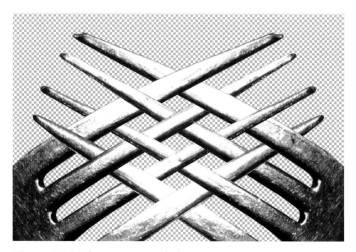

Figure 3.20 *The interwoven forks*

Creating Patterns from Photos: Victorian-Style Patterns

As I teach, I'm often asked questions about Photoshop's capabilities that have little or nothing to do with photography. I've been asked whether Photoshop can be used for creating quilting patterns, digital stained glass that could then be used to create real stained-glass artwork, or even floor-tile patterns.

These are not questions one might expect concerning a program that has its roots in photo correction. The short answer I give these people is simply "Yes, it can." The process may require a bit of work and forethought, but generally if there are color elements involved, then Photoshop can handle the geometry. It is up to the designer or Photoshop pro to work out the details, often with some fairly astounding results.

Frequently techniques used to create a certain type of effect, such as those mentioned in this chapter, are simply variations and combinations of techniques you already know and have applied in other ways. One of the primary differentiating factors between "lefties" and right-brainers is the approach. A technical-minded person will approach Photoshop with a "What can it do?" attitude. Those with an artistic bent tend toward "What if I did this?" Both are solid approaches, but I'd venture to say the latter offers the more gratifying result for the artist.

For this experiment, let's delve into the world of geometric masking. Layer masks can expand the creativity of even the most die-hard left-brainer. By applying strict gradients to layer masks, you can turn *any* photo into a geometric pattern, simulating Victorian patterns or creating seamless backgrounds in just a few steps.

To begin this excursion, open the image `fabric.jpg` (see Figure 3.21).

Figure 3.21 *Fancy fabric photo*

At its present size, this photo could be turned into a seamless background without any alteration to dimensions. Because the premise of this tutorial is to create a Victorian-style pattern, and most patterned cloth squares used in quilting or other such applications are square, this will be as well. Choose Image → Image Size (Alt/Ctrl+I) and deselect the Constrain Proportions checkbox toward the bottom of the dialog box. Enter equal Width and Height values in either the Pixel Dimensions section or the Document Size section to turn the photo into a perfect square. Set Resolution to 300 ppi. See Figure 3.22.

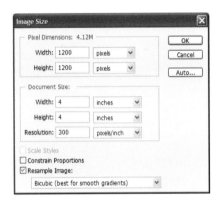

Figure 3.22 Resize the image to perfectly square dimensions.

In Chapter 5, "Effects in the Real World," we will be discussing symmetrical landscaping and patterns in the sky, both of which are variations on the technique about to be performed here. Those techniques use masking as well, so the placement of this tutorial is intentional because of the drastic nature of the masking that takes place. Chapter 5 will offer more refined examples; this technique is a bit radical.

Time to Mask

It's time to set up the Layers panel for the technique. First duplicate the Background layer twice, so that you have three layers in the Layers panel. Select the topmost layer and flip it horizontally (Edit → Transform → Flip Horizontal). Stay with that top layer and add a layer mask by clicking the Add Layer Mask icon at the bottom of the Layers panel. Figure 3.23 shows the Layers panel at this point in the process.

Knowing that black in a mask hides and white reveals layer information, you may have already deduced a bit of what the next step might be. Drawing a stark black-to-white gradient across the mask would basically make the photo appear folded over onto itself. I mentioned, however, that this technique is a bit radical, so the gradient for this layer needs to reflect that.

Click on the mask in the Layers panel to ensure it is active. The foreground and background colors have changed in the toolbar to White/Black, as Photoshop realizes masks can work with only white, black, and shades of gray. After the mask is selected, select the Gradient tool in the toolbar and click directly in the Gradient field in the Options bar to open the Gradient Editor.

Take a look at Figure 3.24. By setting up a straightforward Black/White gradient with very little blending between the two colors, we can create distinct yet seamlessly blended transitions between layers.

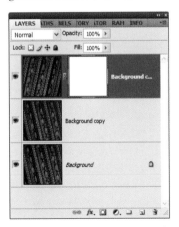

Figure 3.23 The Layers panel as you prepare to work with the first mask

Draw the gradient across the mask from left to right. You will reveal an image that appears reflected on a central vertical plane with very little blending down the central line (see Figure 3.25).

With the topmost layer selected, merge it with the one beneath. You can select the two layers and choose Layer → Merge Layers or use the shortcut ⌘/ Ctrl+E. Duplicate the merged layer and choose Edit → Transform → Flip Vertical. Create a mask for the top layer again, and draw the gradient used before in the mask, only this time starting at the top of the image and drawing the gradient to the bottom edge (see Figure 3.26).

Figure 3.24 Gradient for a radical technique

Figure 3.25 Reflected cloth pattern

Figure 3.26 The start of the masking

Merge the top two layers again. Duplicate the merged layer and choose Edit → Transform → Rotate 90 Degrees CW. Create a mask for the top layer and draw with the gradient in the mask from the top-left corner to the lower-right corner. The Layers panel at this stage will look like Figure 3.27. Merge the top two layers again. We are getting there! (See Figure 3.28.)

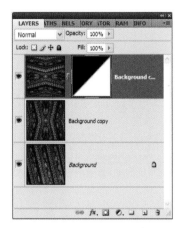

Figure 3.27 *Layers panel at this stage in the process*

Figure 3.28 *Our pattern is starting to take shape.*

Digitized Symmetry

Now we'll see the symmetry start to take shape even further. I know this may seem a bit tedious, but it will take shape in short order.

Duplicate the top layer. Choose Edit → Transform → Flip Horizontal and then Edit → Transform → Flip Vertical. Create the mask again and draw the gradient from the upper-right corner to the lower left. You'll see a cross pattern form from the process at this point. Merge the top two layers again.

Before advancing the masking process, some other characteristics can be added using filters that will enhance the cloth-like quality of the end effect. Duplicate the top layer and choose Filter → Artistic → Cutout. Set Number Of Levels to 8, Edge Simplicity to 4, and Edge Fidelity to 2. This will turn the layer into a drawing more than a photo, which, as I mentioned, will lead to the end effect. Once the settings are in place, click OK (see Figure 3.29 for the pattern at this point).

To add a cloth texture to the pattern, choose Filter → Texture → Texturizer. Set the Texture type to Canvas, Scale to 100%, Relief to 4, and Light to Top. Click OK.

Duplicate the top layer. Choose Edit → Transform → Rotate. On the Options bar, enter **45** in the Set Rotation box. Increase the size of the layer by entering **142%** in both the Width and Height boxes, also found on the Options bar. Accept the transformation. Reduce the opacity of the layer to 60% or so, and merge it with the layer beneath. Figure 3.30 shows the pattern created at this point.

You get the point. You could continue this process to create even more radical designs, generate cloth tiles with stitching for digital quilts, or use as backdrops on anything you desire. One of my favorite things to do is create an action recording the process, and run the action via batch processing on entire folders of images. The pattern will be different with every new photo. You can then save the images in pattern sets for seamless designs used in layer styles and so forth. So save those blurry photos and create new tools for your digital arsenal using this nifty right-brained effect. Figures 3.31 and 3.32 show two designs I created using the same process recorded in an action, with just a few additional embellishments.

Figure 3.29 Cartoon version of the pattern

Figure 3.30 Cloth texture with stylized geometric pattern being realized

Figure 3.31 The same process with a few additional embellishments

Figure 3.32 Another example

Generating Metal Objects and Text

My roots in Photoshop began years ago with text special effects. Text special effects piqued my interest in the software and started me on this journey. Therefore, I would be remiss if I did not include at least a couple of instances of type effects in this book. The rest of this chapter is devoted to text; I hope you enjoy it.

A long time ago, way back in Photoshop 4 (the version I started with), a process for creating stunning type special effects was a bit more tedious than it is today. Generating metal was a drawn-out process that usually had mediocre results. Several versions of Photoshop have arrived on the scene since those early days, and fortunately tools have been added to Photoshop over the course of those years and versions that make text effects such as metal much easier to create in a shorter amount of time.

The technique I am about to demonstrate is simply one way to create metal from scratch. You start with a blank document in Photoshop, and then use it for adding a metallic look to your text. As with many Photoshop techniques, this is only one of the processes that will allow you to create metal. Which technique works best is relative to the artist you ask. It seems in this industry we all have our own way of creating metal or glass or plastic. Often the techniques used will depend on the type of metal you are trying to create or the amount of realism you want to generate. Again, it's all relative, but this is one way you can use a combination of Photoshop tools to generate metallic type.

Heavy Metal Text

Start by creating a blank document 9″ wide by 5″ high, at a resolution of 300 pixels per inch. Set the Background Contents to White and click OK (see Figure 3.33).

For some added flair, draw a gray, black, and white gradient through the image. Set black as the foreground color and, with a large stylized font, type some text. In this example, I've set my font size to 120px. Later I will be placing this on a themed background, so the word *metal* will work fine (see Figure 3.34). Click on the type layer so that the name appears in the layer (see Figure 3.35).

Layer styles are excellent for getting started on the path toward metal. The problem a lot of people have when they create metal effects with type or shapes is that they rely wholly on styles to get their results. True, styles will take you a long way toward creating realistic metal, allowing you to apply bevels, shadings, contours, and so forth. Styles serve as a good foundation, but the following technique will take things a bit further than mere styles.

With the text layer selected, click the Add Layer Style icon at the bottom of the Layers panel. When the Layer Style dialog box pops up, select Bevel And Emboss from the left-hand selections.

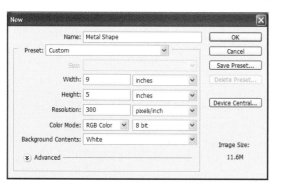

Figure 3.33 *Create a blank document with these settings for the text.*

When I work with styles, as a general rule I'll start with the Bevel And Emboss settings even before I apply color or anything else. In a sense it works like creating a foundation of the building before construction of the walls and interior begins. The bevel allows you to establish how lighting and shadows will affect the face and borders of the text at a foundational level.

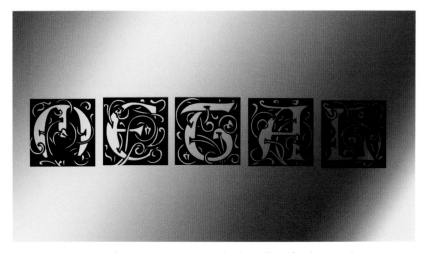

Figure 3.34 *Large black text over a gradual gradient background*

Figure 3.35 *Fire up the forge.*

Figure 3.36 shows the Bevel And Emboss settings portion of the Layer Style dialog box. This screen no longer shows the default settings, as they have been changed to reflect the foundation for the metal text effect.

This is in no way set in stone and this technique may need to be altered later, but right now it represents a good start. The settings to change at this point are as follows:

Depth	460%
Size	18px
Use Global Light	Unchecked
Altitude	25°
Anti-aliased	Checked

With these settings, the type begins its journey to metal. Figure 3.37 shows the effect of altering the bevel on the text, particularly on the edges. They begin to acquire a reflective quality.

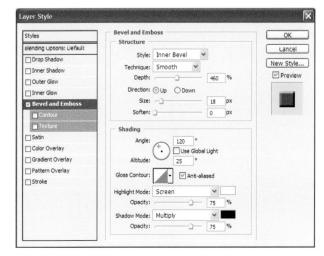

Figure 3.36 *Initial Bevel and Emboss settings of the Layer Style dialog box*

Figure 3.37 *The type is beginning to take on the characteristics of operating in three-dimensional space.*

In the Bevel And Emboss area, there is an icon labeled Gloss Contour that appears as a small version of the Curves dialog box. This setting allows you to apply a contour to the text, which affects how light plays on the surface and edges. Clicking the small arrow next to the Gloss Contour window opens a small icon-view menu where you can select additional contours. Clicking directly in the Contour window allows you to create your own, which is what we will do here. Create a contour that looks like the one shown in Figure 3.38 and click OK.

To further aid the metal effect, change the Highlight color to a very light gray, and the Shadow color to a dark gray, not quite black. Set the opacity for both the Highlight and Shadow to 100%, as shown in Figure 3.39.

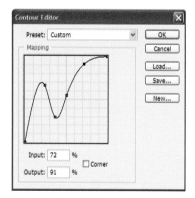

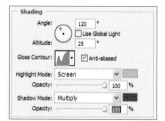

Figure 3.38 *Create a custom Gloss Contour setting.*

Figure 3.39 *Additional adjustments to the Bevel And Emboss settings*

Quick and Painless Variations

You will now quickly step through a series of layer-style adjustment settings. It would take pages to explain each in detail, so I ask that you make the adjustments without the long explanations, instead looking to the effect each setting has on the text and seeing how they play together to generate the metallic shine.

Select Satin from the left-hand Styles menu list. Change the Blend Mode color to light blue. Open the Contour window and choose the Gaussian preset, and then enter the following settings:

Blend Mode	Soft Light
Opacity	50%
Angle	19–20°
Distance	11px
Size	14px
Anti-aliased	Checked
Invert	Checked

Another setting that will help change the text to metal is the Gradient Overlay. This operates like a standard gradient application to a degree, but simply affects the text. Generally a gray-to-white variant gradient works best for metal, and Photoshop has one that works well.

Select the Gradient Overlay setting from the left-hand Styles list. Click the small arrow to the right of the gradient, and then click the small arrow in the upper-right corner of the Gradient Picker that appears. From here you can choose to load additional gradient sets by selecting Load Gradients. Find the gradients that shipped with Photoshop in the Photoshop folder (it should come up by default if you have not changed these settings previously) and choose Metals.grd. Click Load, and the gradients in that gradient set will be available in the Gradient Picker. Open the gradients again and click the gradient labeled Silver when you place the mouse over it. It will be a gray-to-white-to-gray-to-white-to-gray variation. Set up the rest of the Gradient Overlay settings as follows:

Blend Mode	Normal
Opacity	60%
Style	Linear
Align With Layer	Checked
Angle	120°
Scale	100%

How is your text looking so far? It should be gradually becoming more metallic, as shown in Figure 3.40.

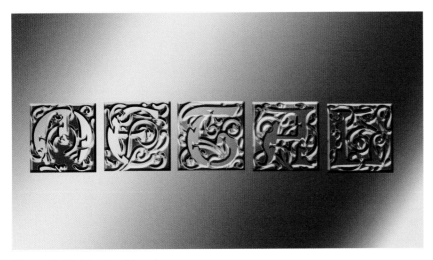

Figure 3.40 Metal taking shape

The Layer Style dialog box also allows you to add a stroke to the text, but you are not restricted to simply using a color: you can also stroke an outline around the text by using a pattern or gradient. Select the Stroke settings from the left side of the dialog box. Change the gradient to the Silver one used in the previous step, and alter the rest of the settings as follows:

Size	6px
Position	Outside
Blend Mode	Normal
Fill Type	Gradient
Gradient	Silver
Style	Linear
Angle	90°
Scale	100%

Figure 3.41 The type is well on its way to metal, simply by adding Layer Style settings.

At this point, the type has taken on a decidedly metallic quality, thanks to a few adjustments to the Layer Style settings. Keep in mind that the actual pixels of the layer have not been altered (*yet!*). While the Layer Style dialog box is still open, click New Style to save these settings for later use. You will be able to apply them with a click of the mouse to any text, photo frame, button, or what have you. Try altering the settings a bit (not now, but later), and save additional variations on this metallic theme. After you have a few, save the layer style set to your hard disk, and you will be able to load and use them at any time via the Styles panel.

After you have the style saved, click OK to apply the style to the text and close the Layer Style dialog box. Your type will closely resemble that shown in Figure 3.41.

Make It Shine

You can further enhance the metallic effect with a series of nondestructive adjustment layers. *Nondestructive* simply means the adjustments are applied to a proxy rather than altering the pixels in a layer.

For instance, let's apply a simple Levels adjustment. First, make a selection in the shape of the text by ⌘/Ctrl-clicking the type layer. At the bottom of the Layers panel, click the Add Adjustment Layer icon and select Levels from the menu. To get a more enriched color variation in the metal, it needs to be darkened a bit. Click on the left slider and move it toward the center, as shown in Figure 3.42, and click OK.

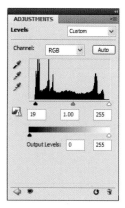

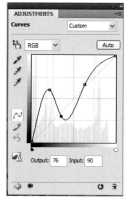

Remember when you changed the Gloss Contour in the Layer Style dialog box? A curve with a similar pattern will help enhance the reflections on the metal. ⌘/Ctrl-click the type layer again to generate the type selection, and again click the Add Adjustment Layer icon at the bottom of the Layers panel. This time select Curves and add and manipulate points on the curve to resemble Figure 3.43. Keep an eye on your type and watch as the metal becomes more enhanced. Click OK to close the Curves dialog box. Your type should closely resemble that shown in Figure 3.44.

Figure 3.42 Adjust the levels with an adjustment layer to darken the text.

Figure 3.43 A Curves adjustment layer makes the metal shine.

Figure 3.44 *Metal type with color reflections*

To remove a bit of the color across the image, you can use a Hue/Saturation adjustment layer. Add one to the image, reducing the Saturation to 33 or so, leaving Hue and Lightness unchanged.

The last adjustment layer to apply for this tutorial is Brightness/Contrast. Select your type again and create a Brightness/Contrast adjustment layer (see Figure 3.45). Watch the type as you move the sliders until you are happy with the shine on your metal type.

Click OK when you are satisfied with the metal your text has become. Figure 3.46 shows the end result of the adjustments. The cool thing about this is you did not have to rasterize the text at any time: all of the settings used to go from plain black text to lustrous metal were nondestructive, whether as a layer style or an adjustment layer. What does that give you? Well, you have maintained the ability to select and change font characteristics (size, spacing) or select the text and change the font to something entirely different. You can even type new words, maintaining the metal effect all the while.

Figure 3.45
*Brightness/Contrast
helps the metal shine.*

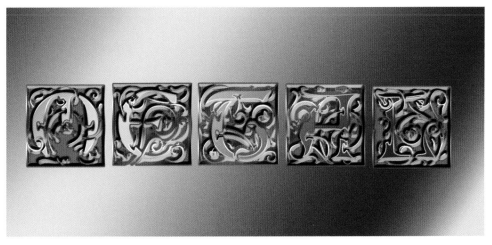

Figure 3.46 *Metallic oiled type, achieved without destroying or altering the text layer*

Now you can simply tweak the settings to generate the style of metal you are looking for. For instance, if I delete the stroke from the original type layer's styles and adjust the Hue And Saturation adjustment layer so that the text is colorized with an amber hue, I can achieve gold in pretty short order, as shown in Figure 3.47. I've placed it on a black backdrop so you can see the effect a bit better.

Figure 3.47 Gold in just a couple of quick steps

Desaturating the text will reveal silver, so on and so forth. This gives you a good foundation on how styles, adjustment layers, and a little imagination can combine to generate some cool metallic effects. Try this on a shape, on a frame, or other type styles. By all means experiment!

Generating Plastic or Glass from Scratch

The same set of tools (layer styles) that started you on your way toward metal type is also extremely useful in generating glass and plastic effects. I've intentionally placed these two techniques together not simply for continuity, but also so you can see how strikingly similar the style settings are between metal and plastic.

For this effect, start with a new blank document filled with white as you did at the beginning of the preceding technique. Insert large black text in a new layer. For this plastic effect, I'm going to use a fat, rounded font to reflect the mood of rounded plastic I'm trying to convey (see Figure 3.48).

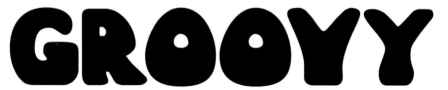

Figure 3.48 A large, rounded font will add to the final plastic effect.

After the font is present and its layer selected, click the Add Layer Style icon at the bottom of the Layers panel and select Bevel And Emboss. As with the metal effect, the bevel and lighting/shadow attached to the settings in this area of the Layer Style dialog box will establish a solid foundation for the plastic effect. Figure 3.49 shows this dialog box with the Bevel And Emboss settings used to create foundational plastic.

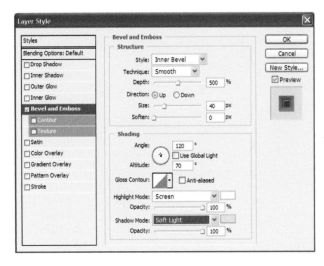

Figure 3.49 Bevel And Emboss will start you on your way to creating cool plastic type.

The default settings for Bevel And Emboss, as with the metal text, need to be altered in order to get a clear plastic shine:

Style	Inner Bevel
Technique	Smooth
Depth	500–550%
Direction	Up
Size	40px
Soften	0px
Angle	120°
Use Global Light	Unchecked
Altitude	70°
Gloss Contour	Linear
Anti-aliased	Unchecked
Highlight Mode	Screen
Highlight Color	White
Highlight Opacity	100%
Shadow Mode	Soft Light
Shadow Color	Light Blue
Shadow Opacity	100%

With these settings, particularly the altitude change to 65–70 degrees, the raised edges of the bevel become clearly reflective, as you can see in Figure 3.50.

Another setting available to get you on your way to plastic type is the Gradient Overlay. Color Overlay works well if you want your type to have a single primary color, but the

Figure 3.50 Altering the Bevel And Emboss settings can make the type highly reflective and take on plastic or glassy characteristics.

gradient allows for multiple colors across the face of the type. Rather than creating a new gradient from scratch this time, select Gradient Overlay from the Styles settings and open the available gradients. Select Orange-Yellow-Orange, one of the default gradients already available to you (see Figure 3.51). Use the following settings:

Blend Mode	Normal
Opacity	100%
Gradient	Orange-Yellow-Orange
Reverse	Unchecked
Style	Linear
Align With Layer	Checked
Angle	125°
Scale	100%

One thing to consider when creating plastic is the transparency factor. If the type you want to create is going to have any transparency, the light will play a bit differently on and inside the object than it would if it were a solid, nontransparent piece. In other words, the inside edges of the text will be lighter than they would be if it were a piece of wood, metal, or even nontransparent plastic.

Figure 3.51 A bit of color, especially a bright color such as orange or yellow, adds to the effect.

To further aid in tricking the eye, you can apply a subtle Inner Glow to softly radiate around the edges, furthering the plastic/semi-transparent illusion. Select Inner Glow from the Styles list and enter the following settings:

Blend Mode	Soft Light
Opacity	75%
Noise	0
Solid Color	Checked, Light Yellow
Technique	Softer
Source	Edge
Choke	0
Size	70px
Contour	Linear
Anti-aliased	Checked
Range	50%
Jitter	0

How is that plastic looking so far? Figure 3.52 shows the type at this stage in the process.

Figure 3.52 Plastic type so far

Now you can work with the opacity to apply transparency to the type. To judge the amount of transparency being applied, you should have something in the background other than stark white. Open the image `blastoff.jpg`. With both the type image and `blastoff.jpg` open, you can select the text image and click on the type layer. Drag that layer over to the `blastoff.jpg` image. You can then select the Move tool or use the arrow keys to position the type on the new image. You may have to use the Transform function to resize the text a bit, or simply select the type and edit the font size as needed.

To reduce transparency of the type layer, move the Opacity slider to 70% in the Layers panel.

The plastic type at 70% opacity should still retain almost all of its reflective qualities but allow you to see the image faintly through the text, as shown in Figure 3.53.

At this point the plastic is effectively complete, although reducing the opacity has a tendency to make the type appear too light. This can be tackled with styles in a couple of ways. You can

Figure 3.53 *The image behind the text will be faintly visible, while the text retains the plastic reflections.*

highlight the edges with an Outer Glow (see Figure 3.54), add a stroke to outline the text (Figure 3.55), and darken the type a bit while maintaining the transparent quality with the Satin setting (Figure 3.56). The variables for enhancing the effect are limited only by your experience with layer styles.

Figure 3.54 *An Outer Glow helps to subtly define the edges.*

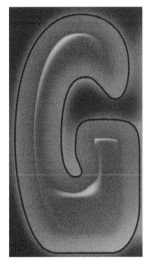

Figure 3.55 *Applying a stroke to the text sharply defines the edges.*

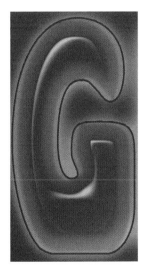

Figure 3.56 *Satin can be used to darken the text while retaining transparency.*

As with the metal text in the previous tutorial, the plastic type was achieved without altering the text layer itself. The type can be selected and changed, resized, warped, and so forth to fit your specific project. Remember to save the layer style when you are finished adjusting your settings by clicking New Style while the Layer Style dialog box is open, then apply the style to the text by clicking OK. The final plastic type image is shown in Figure 3.57.

Figure 3.57 Blastoff!

Summary

I hope you have enjoyed this little jaunt into the realm of special effects. You've made excellent progress, tackling glass spheres, magically intertwining metal objects, forging gold, and even creating geometric Victorian fabrics. Quite a day's work, and that was simply one chapter! You should have masking firmly under your belt at this point, or at least have a solid foundation to build on from this point.

As you move through the following chapters, you will find more project-based sections, somewhat in Chapter 4, "Texture, Color, and Layer Effects," and full throttle in Chapter 5, "Effects in the Real World." You may never have a need to generate glass spheres or gold objects, but the techniques you learned in this chapter will be seen again, albeit applied in other ways. Special effects, for a right-brainer, are stepping-stones to greater creations.

four

Texture, Color, and Layer Effects

My pocket dictionary describes *artistry as an ability attained by study, practice, and observation. I could add imagination to that; once the practice is there and the observations made, if there is no imagination, there is only duplication of what surrounds you or inspired you. A right-brainer will get past this hurdle of imitation and begin creating new forms of art based on old ideas. Likewise, an artist working with Photoshop can create new genres by using tools intended for entirely different purposes. That's what you're going to accomplish in this chapter.*

The images referenced as source files for these techniques can be found in the Chapter 4 Source Files *folder on this book's CD.*

Using Apply Image: Why I Love It

Nearly every person of an artistic bent has a favorite brush, palette, or tool set that they enjoy working with consistently. A woodworker may have a shop filled with all manner of power tools, yet he may prefer to take the edges off the cabinet he is working on with a trusty old handheld planer. Something about that tool *feels* right, and in his mind his work is enhanced by its implementation in the process of creation.

A while back I found that, as I would produce Photoshop-based tutorials for the National Association of Photoshop Professionals (NAPP, at www.photoshopuser.com) or other magazines or websites, I was consistently working with the Apply Image feature at some point in the project. My good friend in the industry, Colin Smith of PhotoshopCAFE.com (http://photoshopcafe.com), still ribs me about it on occasion. He's even made the good-natured comment that someday I may actually realize what it is supposed to be used for.

Apply Image, in short, allows the user to blend the layer and channel of one image (called the source) with the layer and channel of the active image (called the target). In a way this works similarly to altering blending modes of layers in a single document, but in my mind Apply Image gives far more satisfying results and much more control over how the two images interact.

Let's get into this feature and see what it can do.

Enhancing Emotion

In this experiment, you'll use a background texture to bring out even more emotion in a photograph of a woman screaming.

Before you go any further, I have to point out the single most important aspect of Apply Image: both images must have identical pixel dimensions, or this feature will not work. Check the dimensions of your primary photo (pixel width, pixel height); then change the dimensions of the second image to those same settings.

In this demonstration, the image `tantrum.jpg`, found on the book's CD, will be the primary, or target, document (see Figure 4.1). The image `rust_wall.jpg` will be the source (see Figure 4.2).

Ensure that Constrain Proportions is unchecked when you perform the resize operation on `rust_wall.jpg` (see Figure 4.3).

After both photos meet the pixel-dimension limitation, you can proceed with the experiment. Duplicate the Background layer in the `tantrum.jpg` document (see Figure 4.4).

Figure 4.1 I think she's having a bad day.

Figure 4.2 *Streaked and stained with rust*

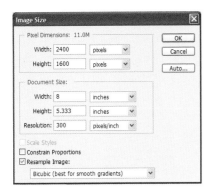

Figure 4.3 *Both images must have the same pixel dimensions before Apply Image can be used.*

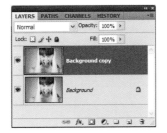

Figure 4.4 *Duplicate the Background layer in the primary, or target, document.*

Apply Image is found in the Image menu. Open the Image menu and select Apply Image from the list.

When the dialog box opens, you will see two primary areas: Source and Target. The target in this instance is the duplicate Background layer just created in the `tantrum.jpg` document. But what you are concerned with here is the Source. If the images do not have identical pixel dimensions, only the target document will appear in the Source menu in the Apply Image dialog box. When both documents have the same pixel dimensions, both will appear in this list. Because you've changed the size of the second document to match the first, open the Source menu and select rust_wall.jpg from the list. You are telling Photoshop to apply the selected layer and channel (in this case the Background layer and RGB channel by default) to the active layer in tantrum.jpg.

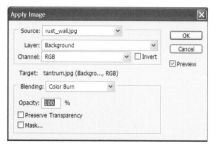

For this initial experiment, the only nondefault setting you will apply is changing the Blending setting to Color Burn. Apply Image, as you can see, allows you to manipulate blending modes just as you would in the Layers panel, only you are affecting far more than simply the layer (see Figure 4.5). After you click OK, the Apply Image settings are applied to the selected layer in the target document. Figure 4.6 shows the results of this first experiment.

Figure 4.5 *Initial Apply Image settings*

Figure 4.6 *Scream, dream, and...*

Granted, this example is a bit dark, and some may even say creepy. I can offer no excuse; much of the art that I create for myself is of a similar bent—not because I enjoy horrific images, but rather the emotion of a well-done dark art piece. What I would like you to see is that you've achieved this stark, emotional piece of art with only two photos and only two changes to settings: an image resize and a blending mode change in the Apply Image dialog box.

This is just the tip of the iceberg! You could drastically alter an effect simply by changing the blending mode in the dialog box. For instance, if you step back in the history one step, open Apply Image again, and then change the Blending to Difference and Opacity to 60% as seen in Figure 4.7, the resulting image is drastically different from the first rendering (see Figure 4.8).

Figure 4.7 *Difference mode in Apply Image*

Figure 4.8 *Changing the blending mode offers a starkly different result.*

Applying a Technical Background

Okay, everyone can relax now as we will move on and use Apply Image with an entirely different genre of digital art. Technical backgrounds and desktop images are popular, whether for websites, posters, or personal use. Apply Image is perfect for these types of photos as well.

Open the images `snuggle.jpg` and `tech.jpg` (see Figures 4.9 and 4.10). Both of these images have already been stylized to a degree: the colors have been changed in the image of the woman and quite a bit of touch-up has already been performed. In the second photo, someone has designed a tech background, probably for use as a splash page for a website.

Remember the rule for using Apply Image: the source document and the target document must have the same pixel dimensions. I reiterate this simply because my e-mail tells me many miss this vital step and wonder why they cannot get Apply Image to work.

Figure 4.9 Nothing like a comfy sweater

Figure 4.10 Digital art background

Ensure that the woman image is active in Photoshop, and choose Image → Apply Image to open the dialog box once again. Retain the settings used previously, with the exception of setting the Source to tech.jpg and changing Blending to Add. You may also opt to play with Scale and Offset: in this instance I set the Scale to 2 and Offset to 1 (see Figure 4.11). Click OK. Figure 4.12 shows the resulting image.

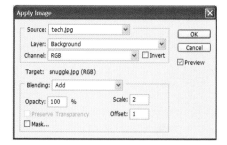

Figure 4.11 New Apply Image settings

If experimentation is a main theme of this book, then the Apply Image feature is one ripe for experimentation. When working with your image blends, try every blending mode Apply Image offers, as well as the Channel settings, working with Masks in the Apply Image dialog box and the Opacity settings. Figure 4.13 shows the same two images blended together with the Blending mode changed to Multiply and the Mask option checked (using the default settings). In Figure 4.14 I've changed the Blending mode to Subtract and also applied the default Mask options. Three variant effects, three different moods… using just two images and a couple of Apply Image setting alterations.

Figure 4.12 *Apply Image for digital-themed desktop images*

Figure 4.13 *You are not restricted to simply one effect.*

Figure 4.14 *I've said this before, I'll say it again: experiment!*

Applying a Montage Effect

You have seen how Apply Image can be used for dark art and digital art pieces, but this is a powerful tool for straightforward photography as well. In the following example I will demonstrate how you can merge two photos for a montage effect popular in all manner of portrait photography, from wedding photos to child photography to yearbooks. The premise is the same as before, but the application is different.

Open the photos babycarosel.jpg and babystare.jpg (see Figures 4.15 and 4.16). For this example of the astounding and incredible Apply Image feature, you will merge these two photos into a stylized collage.

Figure 4.15 Junior's first carousel ride

Figure 4.16 A precious memories pose

The first photo shows a child of two or three trying to figure out if he really enjoys being on that wooden horse without Mom or Dad with him in the saddle. I went through this with my own children, so I absolutely love this shot. The second photo shows a younger version of the same lad, probably in his first year of life and wonder.

Before jumping into Apply Image, note that the color panel of these two images is quite a bit different. You can use Match Color to bring both images closer in the overall color scheme prior to the merge. Ensure that the second photo, babystare.jpg, is active and choose Image → Adjustments → Match Color. Take a look at Figure 4.17. By setting the Source to the first image, the overall hue or panel of the second photo can be altered to better match the tones of the first.

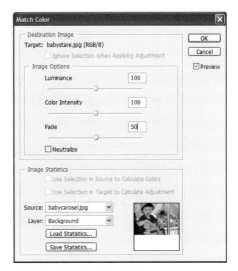

Figure 4.17 *Match Color in action*

Set the Fade value to 50. All I've really adjusted is the color intensity after changing the Source to babycarousel.jpg and selecting Background for the layer the change will be applied to.

After it is set up, click OK.

Click on the second photo (babystare.jpg) and duplicate the Background layer (see Figure 4.18). Alter the size of this image to match the pixel dimensions of the first.

With the color changed and the image resized, Apply Image is ready to be applied. Keep the photo babystare.jpg active and choose Image → Apply Image. Ensure that the Source is set to the first image and that the Blending setting is Multiply (see Figure 4.19). Again, not a lot needs to be changed for this effect to take place.

Figure 4.18 *Resize the second photo and duplicate the Background layer.*

The addition of a layer mask will finish the effect. Rather than use a gradient this time, simply select a black paintbrush and paint over areas of the baby's face where the carousel is showing through, or apply a black-to-white gradient as shown in the example (see Figure 4.20).

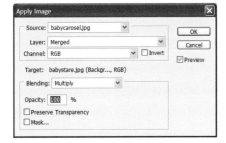

Figure 4.19 *Once more with Apply Image*

Figure 4.20 *Use a layer mask to touch up the image.*

When you are done with the touch-up in the mask, you will have a montage of the child that any parent or grandparent would be proud of (see Figure 4.21).

Figure 4.21 The final montage

This technique has a myriad of applications for photographers, depending on the style of photography and subject matter. I've not even touched on using Apply Image on masks, but teaching the entirety of what Apply Image is capable of is not my intent. I hope that you have seen by my hand and experienced for yourself through these examples what a truly powerful tool this can be, especially in digital art. If you feel you need more practice, keep reading; you will see this powerful feature throughout this text applied in a number of ways.

Adding Color to Black-and-White Images

In some circles, colorizing black-and-white images may be almost as controversial as retouching portraits. But we're not talking about sprucing up classic Hollywood movies like *Casablanca*; we're talking about you, the Photoshop artist, working with images that might become more interesting when you add some color.

There are two simple ways of adding color to black and white: by adding a color cast or by tinting individual colors.

Method 1: Adding a Color Cast

At times, especially when dealing with black-and-white images, just a simple overall color cast can have a striking effect. For this first technique, you will learn how to create a quick tone change on a black-and-white photo.

This technique uses the image `Elderly.jpg` (see Figure 4.22). Find it on the book's CD and open it now.

Figure 4.22 *"What are you looking at?"*

Duplicate the Background layer in the Layers panel. Later you will work with nonde-structive adjustment layers, but for this example you'll be working directly on the layer (actually editing the layer pixels) to ensure that both processes are covered. Rename the Background Copy layer **Aged**, as shown in Figure 4.23.

Choose Image → Adjustments → Hue/Saturation. When the Hue/Saturation dialog box opens, select the Colorize checkbox in the lower-right corner. Then adjust the sliders as shown in Figure 4.24 and click OK.

Figure 4.23 *Duplicate the Background layer and rename the duplicate.*

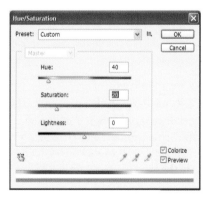

Figure 4.24 *Adjust the Hue/Saturation of the new layer.*

HSB, or Hue, Saturation, and Brightness, are the three fundamental characteristics of color. Hue is the color reflected from or transmitted through an object. Saturation is the strength of that color. Brightness is, of course, how light or dark the color appears. For more information on HSB, refer to the Photoshop Help file on *HSB model.*

This adjustment will give you a general tone resembling sepia (see Figure 4.25). I am not going for an exact sepia effect, but just want to give an earthier feel to the image.

Figure 4.25 *Image resembling sepia (but not quite)*

Painting Selected Areas in a Color Cast

Sometimes one adjustment you make to an image will suggest another. In this case, after I had tinted the image, I decided that painting the eye in a contrasting color would add even more interest. To do that, you'll revisit a technique in Chapter 2, "Techniques for Embellishing Portraits," painting with the Paintbrush tool in Color blending mode. Lighten the reflections in the eye with the Dodge tool. Double-click the foreground color on the toolbar to open the Color Picker dialog box. Find a light brown and click OK.

Select the Paintbrush tool and give it these settings:

Brush:	100
Mode:	Color
Opacity:	70%
Flow:	65%

Notice that I'm using a Soft Round feathered brush. The important thing here is, again, to change the blending mode to Color.

In the Aged layer, paint directly over the iris. Painting over the reflections (white) or pupil (black portion) won't matter; in Color blending mode, whites and blacks are not affected. Only the color information in the painted area, other than black or white, will change.

Sometimes, depending on the color and the thickness of the application of the brush, the tone comes out a bit dark. By going over the colored area with the Dodge tool set to Midtones, you can lighten the color a bit. This adds extra life to the eyes; depending on how strongly you apply the tool, the eye can take on a mystical quality, burning with inner life. Select the Dodge tool and set these options:

Brush	44
Range	Midtones
Exposure	32%

Apply the Dodge tool to the iris, brightening the midtones. Don't linger too long in one spot, but just give the tool a general swipe around the perimeter of the pupil.

Occasionally you may desire a more vibrant or shocking color, and a simple reapplication of the Paintbrush tool with a different hue can have a striking effect.

For instance, change the foreground color again, this time using a yellowing green. Select the Paintbrush tool again and, using the same options set up previously, paint over the iris. This setting changes the hue of the eye, contrasting the eye with the overall tone of the rest of the image (see Figure 4.26).

Figure 4.26 *Youthful spark in a wizened face?*

Method 2: Re-creating the Hand-Tinted Look

Not every black-and-white image can be colored by something as basic as a Hue/Saturation adjustment and some painting. Some images require a bit more to bring out natural tones.

I'm not certain this tinting technique renders what you might call natural tones, however. This technique is more in the style of methods used years ago to color photographs of their time. Color film wasn't commonplace 60-plus years ago (yes, I realize that is an understatement), so much of the color seen in old photos was added later. It gives the photos a retro feel, and I love retro.

Take a look at the image BW-Portrait.jpg (see Figure 4.27). Is that a cute kid or what? It is somehow hard to envision that this youngster would now most likely be in his seventies.

The first layer you will work on will correct the frame, giving it an aged-paper feel. Create two copies of the Background layer and make the topmost copy invisible. Select the layer just above the original background.

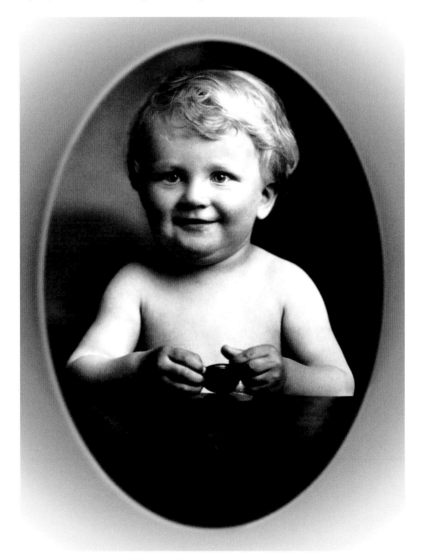

Figure 4.27 Somebody's grandpa

I often switch back and forth between creating adjustment layers (which applies the adjustment to all the layers beneath it) and applying adjustments directly to a specific layer. If I don't want the adjustment to be destructive, then an adjustment layer works perfectly. If I don't care that the pixels on the layer are altered, or if I don't want the change to apply to the layers beneath, then I may apply the adjustment directly to the layer.

In this instance, you're going to use an adjustment layer. Create a new Hue/Saturation adjustment layer and move the sliders as shown in Figure 4.28. This will give the image a sepia appearance, implying age.

Select the topmost layer; this will be the second duplicate of the background created earlier. Create a mask for the layer. Using a black brush with the opacity for the brush set to 60%, paint around the frame edges in the mask. This will hide the black-and-white frame and reveal the colored frame beneath. The child will remain without color to this point (see Figure 4.29).

If you revealed a portion of the background also, don't worry about it in this case. The overall effect is to be one of age, so having the brown show through on the photo backdrop is permissible. The main goal is that the boy still be grayscale (see Figure 4.30).

Figure 4.28 *Hue/Saturation adjustment*

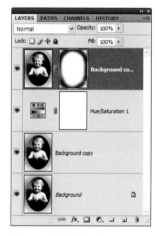

Figure 4.29 *Mask away the black-and-white frame.*

Figure 4.30 *Child in grayscale*

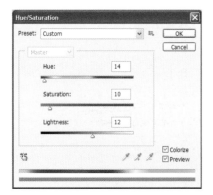

You will be making another Hue/Saturation adjustment but this time to the actual layer. Choose Image → Adjustments → Hue/Saturation and enter the values shown in Figure 4.31. Click OK. This is going to give the child some color, albeit faint.

Create a new layer and change the blending mode to Color. As you should be well familiar with by now, select a foreground color for the hair and paint over the hair with the Paintbrush tool in that layer. If the hair appears too well colored, simply lower the opacity of the layer. After the hair has been tinted, change the foreground color again, this time to a tone that will likely match his skin color (see Figure 4.32). In the same layer as the hair color, paint over the skin areas of the child (see Figure 4.33).

Figure 4.31 *Hue/Saturation values—again*

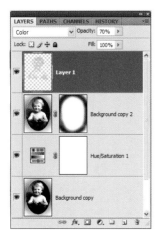

Figure 4.32 *Coloring the hair and skin*

Figure 4.33 *Black and white slowly comes to life.*

Continue coloring in this layer, but change the foreground color to red to add some rose to the boy's cheeks. Switch to a light blue and paint over the irises—you should be well versed in this by now! Note that there may be some bleeding over of color beyond the borders of the hair and so forth. If you take a close look at this style of photograph, you will find that was quite common and adds to the effect (as long as it isn't overdone).

For the final step, add some color to the table. Select a dark brown/red for the foreground color. Create a new layer at the top of the layer stack and set the blending mode to Overlay (see Figure 4.34). Now simply paint over the table surface. Figure 4.35 shows the final image, complete with a newly varnished table and the boy's reflection off the surface.

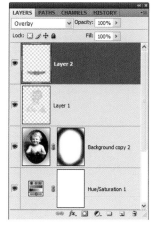

Figure 4.34 *Painting the tabletop*

Figure 4.35 *Grandpa's baby photo, fully restored*

If you aren't sure what to do with a technique like this, I submit to you that photo restoration and coloring is becoming popular, especially among people of the older generations. You might be able to work a little digital magic and make an elder smile—that is reward in itself.

We'll now move on to another exercise in painting with Photoshop, although one markedly different than the recoloring processes demonstrated so far. Next on the agenda: applying old paint to a rough texture.

Using Textures and Displacement Maps

Most of the work you've seen in this book consists of generating photorealistic effects. Earlier in this chapter you used Apply Image and colorizing to create photorealistic effects. You are now going to add textures and displacement maps to your toolbox. Other areas of this book cover these subjects, to be sure; for this portion I'd like to give them a tighter focus and show what can be done with each.

In the experiments that follow, you will learn to apply digital paint to a rough surface, such as a brick wall. The paint will appear faded and aged, and even conform to the wall's indents and raised areas. The second technique utilizes a similar process, but instead of paint you will combine real-world textures with human skin. Sounds creepy, but the effect can be stunning!

Aged Paint on a Rough Surface

Texture photos are an excellent resource for digital art, as shown in the first Apply Image exercise. They give photos character that didn't exist previously, especially for dark or grunge effects. Let's say, however, you want an effect performed *on* a texture, rather than *with* a texture. An example of what I mean is the application of paint on a surface where none existed before. Applying color is no difficult task, but getting the paint to conform to the shapes and contours in the texture—well, that takes a little work—not hard work, mind you, but a process nonetheless. Once again, Photoshop is ready, willing, and able to meet the need.

Open the image `bricks.jpg` (see Figure 4.36).

Figure 4.36 Another brick in the wall

The filter of choice to get a color or pattern to conform to the contours of the wall is the Displace filter. Displace uses a displacement map consisting of white, black, and gray to produce positive and negative shifts in pixels to the image. For instance, a 0 (zero) value will produce the maximum negative shift, 255 the maximum positive shift, and a gray 128 value will offer no change. You have seen this filter in action once already when you applied the map to the man's skin in Chapter 1, "Tools for Building Your Masterpiece," but another look is warranted, especially for those unfamiliar or unpracticed with its operation. This is one powerful tool to have in your digital toolbox.

Displacement maps for the type of application you will be using them for are created by using duplicates of channels, or rather a channel, with high contrast between the lights in the darks. In Figure 4.37, I duplicated the blue channel because it gives me the highest contrast. You can select each channel one at a time and judge this yourself visually, which is what I've done here. The channel will now be used to create a displacement map.

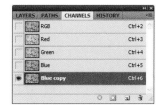

Figure 4.37 The blue channel will be used as the foundation for the displacement map.

With the copy channel selected, a Brightness/Contrast adjustment can be performed on it to further increase the contrast between the lights in the darks. This will give you better displacement because you are moving the values away from the center (128) and toward 0 and 255.

Figure 4.38 shows my setting; I have left Brightness alone but increased Contrast to +40. The Preview checkbox is selected to gauge the amount of contrast being applied visually.

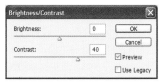

Figure 4.38 Brightness/ Contrast is applied to further separate the lights and the darks.

The next step employs the Gaussian Blur filter. You will apply this filter to the copy channel to make the blend between whites, grays, and blacks more gradual. As shown in Figure 4.39, set the Radius value of the blur to 10 pixels; the result can be seen in the Document window when Preview is checked. You're not looking for a total blur. You want some details and contours to still be present; they just need to be softened for when Displace is run.

Let's take a quick look at the original wall photo before you go any further (see Figure 4.40). Note the cracks in the wall, the separation of the bricks from the mortar in between, and the variation between the light and dark areas. For this experiment, I will demonstrate how to paint some of the bricks without having to paint the mortar or the other lighter surfaces. Is this even possible? You bet it is, and it's so simple you won't believe your eyes.

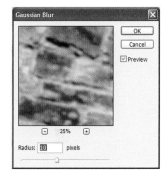

Figure 4.39 Apply a Gaussian blur to the duplicate channel.

Figure 4.40 One more look at the wall

Figure 4.41 *The map channel is saved as its own image.*

First let's finish the map. The map itself needs to be safe and secure as its own file. With the duplicate blue channel selected, right-click (or navigate via the channel's menu) and select Duplicate Channel. Names are not important for this example, but if you do this for your own work you may want to name a new channel appropriately. The primary point here is to change the Document setting under Destination to New (see Figure 4.41). Click OK. A copy of the channel will appear on the desktop as a new image. Save this image to your hard disk in a place where you can find it shortly, as it will come into use very soon. Also, delete the duplicate blue channel in the original wall photo.

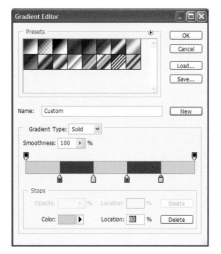

Figure 4.42 *A gradient will serve as the paint on the bricks.*

It's time to apply color to this thing. Return to the original document and create a new layer. Fill the layer with a gradient created by using yellow and gray alternating colors with no blurred separation between the two. Fill the layer diagonally. I'm not going to explain the process of creating a gradient, simply because in this case color doesn't matter and I've demonstrated gradient creation elsewhere in the book. You could use a photo rather than color, so this is just an example (see Figure 4.42).

Fill the new layer with the gradient, starting in the upper-left corner and drawing the gradient to the lower-right corner. With the gradient-filled layer selected, you can go ahead and access the Displace filter. Choose Filter → Distort → Displace. In the dialog box that appears, set Horizontal Scale to 10 and Vertical Scale to 10. In the Displacement Map section, select Stretch To Fit, and in the Undefined Areas section, select Wrap Around; then click OK (see Figure 4.43). Photoshop will ask you to find the displacement map to use; navigate to the map you just created, select it, and click OK. After you do this, the selected layer will distort based on the color values of the map, from 0 to 255, making the pattern appear to conform to the contours of the wall.

Figure 4.43 *Enter the settings for the Displace filter.*

After running the Displacement filter and using the map, on the gradient layer I created the straight lines separating my colors and distorted them to conform with the lights and the darks in the wall, as shown in Figure 4.44.

Next you'll want to ensure that the wall can be seen beneath the paint. Change the blending mode of the top layer to Soft Light to make the bricks visible once again (see Figure 4.45).

Figure 4.44 *After the map is applied to the layer, the layer will distort to match the contours and colors of the wall image.*

Figure 4.45 *Blending-mode change*

The next step in the process concerns wiping away color, or paint, from specific areas of the wall and leaving it on others. For this example I want you to apply yellow paint only to the bricks, and leave the white and gray mortar untouched. I don't want the gray paint, or the gray areas of the gradient, to show up either. The effect I am looking for is of a wall that had yellow bars painted on it at one time but then was covered by the mortar. Over time, the mortar has chipped away, revealing the painted bricks once again.

The simplest Photoshop feature that will render the most realistic result, at least in my experience, is Blend If. The Blend If settings are found for each layer in the Layer Style settings for that layer under Blending Options. To change the Blend If settings for the gradient layer, click on the layer in the Layers panel (it should be active still) and open that layer's layer styles. When the Layer Style dialog box opens, select Blending Options at the top of the list on the left-hand side. The Blending Options section in the center of the dialog box will display Blending Mode (in this case Soft Light, reflecting the setting you changed earlier), the Opacity setting of the layer, the Advanced Blending settings (the Fill Opacity can be seen here also), and then the Blend If settings at the bottom.

Whereas the displacement map allows you to distort the layer based on color information, Blend If lets you manipulate the visibility of colors based on the color information of

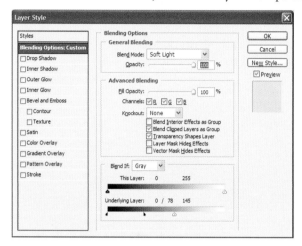

this layer and the layers beneath. Basically you will be telling Photoshop which colors can be visible and which invisible based on the colors in the layer beneath. Figure 4.46 shows the Layer Style dialog box with Blend If affecting the gray tones. By manipulating the sliders beneath the This Layer field and the Underlying Layer field, you can adjust the visibility of the gray color in the gradient. To separate the paired sliders, hold down the Option/Alt key and click to split the slider with the mouse. The combination you see in this figure effectively lights the gray away in all areas of the layer. The color information is still in the layer—it has simply been rendered invisible by this adjustment.

Figure 4.46 The first Blend If alteration

Figure 4.47 This Blend If adjustment leaves the yellow only on the bricks, wiping it away from the mortar.

The adjustment shown in Figure 4.47 retains the yellow on the bricks but effectively lifts it from the mortar.

Figure 4.48 shows the final image. Note that the paint is primarily on the bricks, with a couple of spots on the mortar, and no trace of gray to be found. Because of the displacement map, the paint conforms to the contours of the brick, and the Soft Light blending mode allows you to see the brick beneath the paint. When working for photorealism, no one filter or technique is going to get satisfying results—99.9 percent of the time it will take combinations of techniques to get a realistic result. This combination allows you to fool the eye so the viewer will assume that it's natural rather than a fabrication. When you can do that, you'll know the satisfaction that digital artists, in particular photorealistic artists, thrive on.

Figure 4.48 The mortar has fallen away, revealing an old paint job.

Adding Real-World Texture to Skin

You've seen the result of using displacement maps (and a couple of other tools) for applying paint to a wall in a photorealistic way. Right-brainers are rarely satisfied with simply generating photorealism of realistic objects. Right-brainers are more prone to stretching the boundaries, creating photorealism where none should exist. For example, the digital artists who visit websites such as deviantART (www.deviantart.com) use texturing on the human form to evoke emotion or shock value from their work.

In this example, I will demonstrate one way to apply real-world textures to human skin. For those of you with no interest in dark art, consider this an exercise in the imagination. You might easily perform the same technique by applying steel textures to a glass bottle, aging a billboard, or what have you.

Open the images `calm.jpg` and `cracked.jpg` (see Figures 4.49 and 4.50).

Figure 4.49 *A serene close-up*   *Figure 4.50* *Cracked-marble texture*

On the image of the woman, select the channel with the best separation and contrast between the lights and the darks, as you learned in the previous exercise, and create a displacement map. Remember to apply the blur as you did before (see Figure 4.51), and save a duplicate of the new channel to your hard disk. Delete the extra channel from the image of the woman, and select the RGB channel to return it to normal (see Figure 4.52).

Copy and paste the texture photo into `calm.jpg`. Use the Transform commands to adjust the size of the layer to encompass the entire layer. Apply the Displace filter by using the displacement map just created with the Displace settings shown in Figure 4.53.

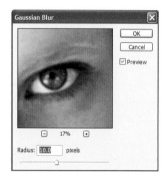

Figure 4.51 Gaussian blur for the displacement map

Figure 4.52 Return `calm.jpg` *to its original state.*

Figure 4.53 Displace filter settings

Let's try something a bit different before you make the leap to the final image. With the textured layer displaced and ready to be affixed to the face, you have some room for experimentation. First, duplicate the texture layer and shut off the topmost version. Next, select Layer 1 and change the blending mode to Hard Light. Select the top layer, turning it on, and change the blending mode to Difference (see Figure 4.54). Create a Curves adjustment layer and alter the curve to increase the brightness level of the dark areas. Watch the change in the image when you alter the curve. Figure 4.55 shows an example I came up with using this technique.

Figure 4.54 Set the blending mode for the first texture layer to Hard Light and the second to Difference.

Figure 4.55 New image with a Curves adjustment added

As I've demonstrated before, a technique such as this is usually only a couple of quick steps away from something entirely different—but equally interesting as or even better than the first rendering. Because you started this adventure attempting to combine texture with skin semi-photorealistically, the next step will get you to that destination.

Shut off the Difference layer and delete the Curves adjustment layer. Select the first texture layer and change the blending mode to Multiply. This will affix the texture to the skin (see Figure 4.56). When I'm working with this technique, I tend to stay away from texturing the "soft areas" of the face, such as the eyes and mouth. Again, a mask with black paint applied to these areas will wipe the texture away, revealing the unaltered eye and eyelashes. Figure 4.57 shows the resulting textured face.

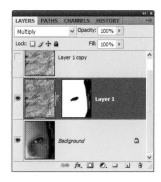

Figure 4.56 Manipulating the layers for an entirely different effect

Figure 4.57 Texture mapped to the face

As I close this section on textures and displacement maps, I want to leave you with a couple of variations that I created for personal enjoyment and that fit the same theme (see Figures 4.58 and 4.59). Both images use the same techniques you saw in this section (using different images), with only slight variations in technique applied to fill out the final piece. If you have no desire to texture faces, I can understand. Simply keep in mind that these same processes can be used in any number of ways. The application is up to your imagination.

Figure 4.58 *The face of age*

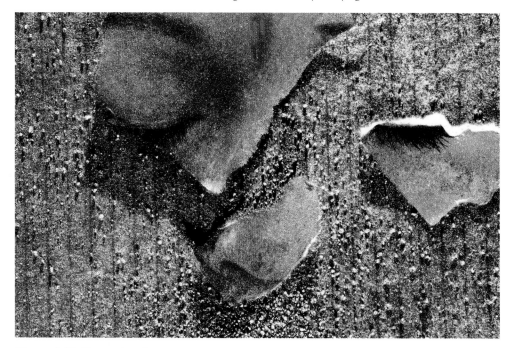

Figure 4.59 *Tattered and torn*

Lightening, Darkening, and Coloring

You can alter photographs of people, objects, animals, and scenery, but that is certainly not the extent of what Photoshop is capable of correcting or, as in the previous exercise, damaging. The art of the great masters can be corrected, cleaned, and enhanced also. You cannot use Photoshop to dress up the actual Mona Lisa, but you can use it to dress up a copy with lightening, darkening, and coloring techniques in Photoshop.

Open the image `chapel.jpg` (see Figure 4.60).

Figure 4.60 Painting from a master, with a nasty blue cast

Here is a small sample of one of the most famous paintings on the planet. Let's see if you can dress this up a tad. Not having visited Europe, I can't say whether the Sistine Chapel has a blue cast to its ceiling. However, this photograph of that ceiling clearly has a blue cast. The color in the hands, the color of the background—let's perform a correction that would hopefully make Michelangelo proud. Duplicate the Background layer (see Figure 4.61).

In this step you're going to do something a bit different. We will touch on something you haven't worked with in this book yet: the Channel Mixer. This will allow you to get better contrast by turning the layer that you're working on into a high-quality grayscale version of the original. You can physically set the percentage contribution for each color channel. With the Channel Mixer, you're not actually adding color information or altering color information in your image, but rather are adding and subtracting grayscale data from a source channel to a targeted channel. The result is a crisper grayscale version of the photo, which translates to lighter lights, darker darks, and more vibrant color.

Figure 4.61 Begin by duplicating the Background layer.

Okay, that may seem a bit vague; let's just walk through the process and see what happens. Choose Image → Adjustments → Channel Mixer and open the dialog box. Select the Monochrome check box in the lower-left corner and set Output Channel to Gray. Increase the amount of red in the Source Channels section to 90%, Green to 30%, and Blue to 28%. Leave Contrast at 0 and click OK (see Figure 4.62). You now have a monochrome, or grayscale, version of the painting in that Background Copy layer. Set the blending mode to Overlay.

Figure 4.62 *Working with the Channel Mixer*

Take a look at Figure 4.63. This simple adjustment and blending-mode change has increased intensity of the color and definition of lines tenfold. By adding a new layer with the blending mode set to Color, you can enhance the color of the skin as you did in Chapter 2 when colorizing hair by selecting skin tone and applying it over the hands. Changing the blending mode of that Background Copy layer to Normal (see Figure 4.64) will wipe away the blue on the background and leave you with your own version of this famous painting, with just the hands in color and the backdrop in shades of black, white, and gray (see Figure 4.65).

I have demonstrated enhancing a painting in this example, but this technique most certainly works on photographs as well. Remember to focus not on what is being worked on, but on how you might use these techniques in other genres or in areas of correction specific to your interest or need. Photoshop is great that way. After you have mastered a technique, or even acquired rudimentary knowledge of a process of correction or alteration, Photoshop releases creative license to you. Digital art is not about the software, but about you realizing the vision in your mind.

Figure 4.63 *Whites, darks, and color enhanced*

Figure 4.64 *Skin colorization and background-color removal*

Figure 4.65 *A new color panel for an old, famous classic*

Summary

We've run quite a course in this chapter, utilizing Photoshop to artistically enhance or alter photos that can be used in a wide variety of ways: from the relatively tame blending or recoloring of personal photos to the wild, decidedly artsy (and occasionally dark) neighborhood of combining textures with people. These areas can make the digital artistry in photographers shine, separating them from the competition in ways that could add diversity to their portfolio.

In the next chapter we'll continue this theme, taking a turn away from portraits and dealing with scenes from nature and the urban world.

five

Effects in the Real World

As children, we all looked up *at the clouds and saw misty ships, crocodiles, or riders on horseback. Who am I kidding? I still do it frequently. It may seem fanciful, but to me these cloud shapes are examples of how patterns repeat in nature. Over the past few years, the emerging science of fractals—colorful patterns generated by mathematical formulae that repeat endlessly—has begun to show us the significance of these patterns. All things physical seem to be tied to similar mathematical formulas.*

Our world consists of similar (in many cases identical) patterns and formulae, whether calculating the rotation of solar systems around a central point or studying the arc of a single rotation of a strand of DNA. The universe is a wondrous combination of fractals built with a specific design in mind, using math as the foundation to tie all things together and dictate the boundaries that keep everything in operation. To those who stand too close to the canvas, it may seem chaotic and random. Stepping back, you can see the entire picture and begin to appreciate what the designer, as artist, envisioned when the first stroke of paint was lovingly applied.

In this chapter we'll be looking at effects that take symmetry to the extreme, manipulating landscapes and sky scenes to find some of those hidden patterns. We'll also delve into light, reflections, and mood alterations with a few nifty Photoshop CS4 alterations and tweaks. Let's see if we can't lend nature a hand in generating scenes that "should have been."

The images referenced as source files for these techniques can be found in the Chapter 5 Source Files *folder on this book's CD.*

Symmetrical Landscaping

I'm of the mind that patterns in nature are hardly random, but demonstrate incredible order rather than chaotic happenstance. The laws of thermodynamics tell us that the universe is gradually decaying to a more chaotic state, but Photoshop can assist digital artists in creating order in their landscapes. In Chapter 1, "Tools for Building Your Masterpiece," you experimented with masks to attain exaggerated symmetry. What happens when these same techniques (or strikingly similar techniques, at least) are applied to nature?

Before proceeding, let me make a personal aside. Although the technique you are about to perform is also seen elsewhere in this book (albeit applied differently), I'm including it here as well to reiterate a point: applying a process to varied scenes, models, and image types can produce entirely different artistic ends. The focus is not on the process, but rather on using Photoshop imaginatively and perhaps helping to get those creative juices flowing. Some people prefer working with a human canvas, and some prefer working with nature. This technique is for the latter photographer.

Symmetry in the Sky

The twilight of the day is often a photographer's favorite time to grab a camera and run for the hills. Living in Montana, I am on the receiving end of spectacular sunsets over the mountains, whether the transitions of orange to deep blue in summertime or the shift to frosty grays in the wintertime as the clouds hang heavy with snow. In this technique we'll add our own symmetry to a sunset landscape and see what scenes of wonder are revealed.

Open the image Horizon.tif from the Chapter 5 Source Files folder on this book's CD. Figure 5.1 shows the scene at the start: a beautiful sunset. The photo appears to have been taken shortly after a cloudburst. The storm has passed, and you can almost smell the damp grass and moist earth.

Figure 5.1 Sunset after rain

Figure 5.2 *Add a layer mask to the flipped layer.*

To add a bit of exaggerated symmetry, the picture can be folded over onto itself, with the help of a gradient applied to a layer mask.

Duplicate the Background layer. With the new layer selected, choose Edit → Transform → Flip Horizontal. After the layer has been flipped, click the Add Layer Mask icon (see Figure 5.2).

If you saved the gradient created during the process in Chapter 1, you may use it again here. If not, select the Gradient tool and create a black-to-white gradient with a 2% separation in the center, moving the Black color stop to 49% and the White color stop to 51%. This 2% separation allows for a narrow blended area between the colors. If both were set to 50%, the gradient would create a distinct line through the center of the photo when applied to the mask. The gradual transition from black to white, although narrow, will fool the eye just enough to suit our purposes here. To see the gradient settings, take a look at Figure 5.3. After the gradient is created, you can click New to add it to the loaded gradients and then click OK.

With the gradient created and selected, ensure that the mask is active and draw the gradient across the mask, from the left edge of the photo to the right. Holding down the Shift key will allow you to keep a steady hand and maintain a straight gradient (see Figure 5.4).

Figure 5.5 shows the result of the gradient applied to the mask, revealing a landscape that is "absolute" in its symmetry. Everything from the clouds to the foreground grass is reflected perfectly. If you look closely and use a bit of imagination, you can almost see faces in the foreground grass!

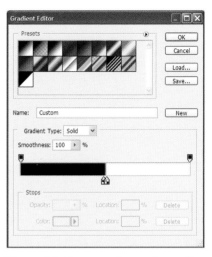

Figure 5.3 *Create and save the gradient.*

Figure 5.4 *Apply the gradient to the mask.*

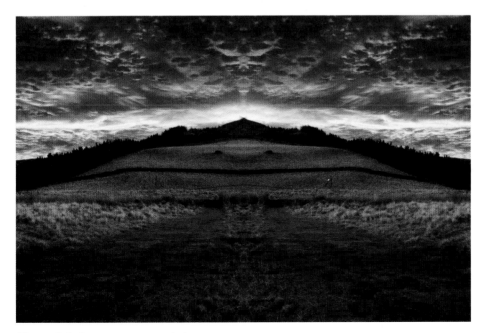

Figure 5.5 *A new scene revealed*

The original photo had a crossroads-style sign in the foreground that would be an excellent addition to the scene. Also, there is another landscape alternative that you could use. To take a look at it, simply invert the colors in the mask (Image → Adjustments → Invert). By swapping the black and white in the mask (see Figure 5.6), a new scene is revealed. The sign is again present, and now a rough stone-bordered path appears to be leading to a cloven hill (see Figure 5.7).

Figure 5.6 Invert the mask colors.

The effect thus far has basically generated a reflection, which is a bit too unnatural. Portions of the scene can be removed (or rather returned to their original state) while maintaining the odd mirroring over much of the photo. Simply painting with a black brush (see Figure 5.8) in the layer mask over select areas of the photo can have dramatic results.

Figure 5.7 Path to a cloven hill

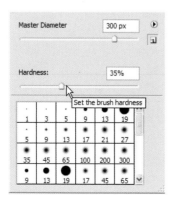

Figure 5.8 Set up a brush for additional painting in the mask.

In this example, you really need only a single sign to direct the way through this strange landscape. Working within the mask, you could paint black over the sign on the left side of the photo to reveal the original grass beneath. You could also opt to paint over the clouds and the hill's horizon to show the area where the sun is hitting the brightest. Another point in the mask you may wish to correct is the center of the cloven hill. Painting in the mask here will remove the gradual fade (see Figure 5.9).

The final scene maintains the unnatural symmetry while carrying on the illusion that this could happen in nature (see Figure 5.10). Hiding the sign and revealing a few original characteristics on the left side of the photo should give viewers pause: are they really seeing what they think they are seeing? What wonders Photoshop and a little imagination can accomplish.

In the next technique we'll look to the heavens again and apply similar alterations. This technique looks at a different cloud-formation type, and should garner an entirely different feeling. Remember those fanciful cloud castles from your childhood as we look into sky symmetry once more.

Figure 5.9 *Hide portions of the top layer by adding black to the mask.*

Figure 5.10 *Pathway revealed by Photoshop and the imagination*

Patterns in the Sky

I have an affinity for performing the symmetrical masking technique on cloud formations. As a boy growing up in central Montana, I would watch distant puffs of white build and grow into towering thunderheads in the summer. Watching nature in action, weather in particular, is a fascination I will take to my grave—of this I'm certain.

In this example the technique will be much the same as before, but this time the foreground scene will remain unaltered and only the cloud formation will change. Open the image clouds1.jpg found on this book's CD (see Figure 5.11).

Figure 5.11 *Plains country horizon*

As before, duplicate the Background layer. Create a mask, and with the gradient saved in the previous exercise, draw the gradient across the mask from the left border to the right (see Figure 5.12). The resulting image is shown in Figure 5.13.

Figure 5.12 *Apply the same gradient settings as before to the new layer mask.*

Returning to the original foreground scene is a simple matter; I would wager that you have already deduced how to accomplish this. That's right: fill in the lower portion of the mask with black. Because this photo has a relatively straight horizon, creating a selection with the Rectangular Marquee tool in the mask (see Figure 5.14) and filling the selection with black (see Figure 5.15) will effectively render a pattern in the clouds without altering the foreground. Some soft painting in the mask on the right-hand side will allow for the addition of a few characteristics from the original, such as the trees or a soft casting of sunshine on the ridge. Figure 5.16 shows the final image.

Figure 5.13 *An interesting intersection*

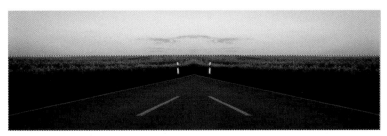

Figure 5.14 *Select the lower portion of the mask to just above the horizon.*

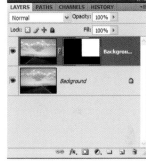

Figure 5.15 *Fill the selection in the mask with black.*

Figure 5.16 *Patterns in the sky*

Although I am not demonstrating it in this example, feel free to apply black or white paint to the mask in other spots among the clouds to reduce the amount of symmetry. If this were a recipe book, it would read "season to taste."

Once again, this is only one version of the scene. There is another lurking here, and it can be discovered simply by selecting the mask and inverting the colors. When this is done, an entirely different cloud formation is revealed, and the road changes direction as well (see Figure 5.17).

Before we move on to the effects we see in nature, let's tackle this sky effect one more time, only with this pass we'll add one of my favorite Photoshop CS4 tricks: Apply Image.

Figure 5.17 An alternate view

Nature Patterns: Apply Image

As discussed in Chapter 4, "Texture, Color, and Layer Effects," Apply Image is one of my absolutely favorite tools in the realm of Photoshop. I will not go into yet another diatribe praising this incredible, life-changing feature (it has been known to reduce hair loss, enhance self-esteem, and reverse ozone depletion), although in my honest opinion it is certainly warranted.

Apply Image can be used to generate patterned scenes as well. For this example, open the photo `clouds2.jpg` from the book's CD (see Figure 5.18). Here you have a tranquil sunset scene over the ocean, something I took for granted in my Navy days. Not to dismiss the beauty of sunsets in the Rockies, but there is something surreal about an ocean twilight. And in this case, you can create your own sunset with a symmetrical, surreal twist.

As before, duplicate the Background layer and flip it (see Figure 5.19). This time the effect will be created without a mask: you will use Apply Image on this layer to achieve the new scene. Choose Image → Apply Image. When the dialog box opens, set the Source to `clouds2.jpg`. You can use the original image (that is, the unflipped Background layer) and blend it with the flipped layer to get the scene to meld. Set the Layer to Background and change the blending mode to Overlay (see Figure 5.20). Click OK.

Figure 5.18 *Sunset on the water*

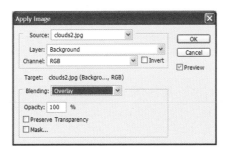

Figure 5.19 *Duplicate the Background layer; no mask this time.*   *Figure 5.20* *Apply Image settings*

The result gives you the mirrored scene again, this time with the colors enriched by the Overlay blending mode (see Figure 5.21). In this example, because Apply Image was the tool of choice rather than a mask, portions of the scene cannot be hidden. However, if you were to create a mask for this layer, you could see what painting with black/white or gray would do to the final shot. By ghosting the layer, you can get a feel for the hidden image, or rather what will be revealed when the process is complete.

Figure 5.21 *Symmetry in the sunset*

Creating a Neon Reflection on Water

When I first considered the following piece, I imagined a cobblestone street or walkway with a few stones removed, the recessed area serving as a puddle of water. But then I found this access.jpg image (see Figure 5.22) with the cover plate recessed into the surrounding walkway. The way my mind works, I thought, "Hey, that would be cool if it were turned into a reflective puddle." Don't ask me why I thought that, but it did enter my mind. You can use that recessed area to create a half inch of semitransparent water with a neon reflection inside.

Figure 5.22 *Recessed cover plate in a sidewalk*

Open access.jpg from the book's CD to start this exercise.

Duplicate the Background layer of access.jpg. Select the Polygonal Lasso and create a selection around the cover (see Figure 5.23). The area to the top left of the selection will be somewhat jagged, because the broken stones around the plate are more evident. You need not include the broken recesses in the selection, but don't simply create a straight-lined selection in this area either.

Move the selected plate to its own layer by choosing Layer → New → Layer Via Cut.

Next you will prepare the neon image to use as the puddle reflection. Open the image neon.jpg (see Figure 5.24). Select the entire image, copy it, and paste it into its own layer in the sidewalk image. Flip the image (it will be a reflection, so it needs to be reversed) by choosing Edit → Transform → Flip Horizontal.

Figure 5.23 Selection of the cover plate

Figure 5.24 I love the blues.

Reduce the scale of the new layer to fit over the plate area. If the plate extends beyond the edges of the neon layer's pixels, don't fret; that will be corrected in short order (see Figure 5.25).

Now use the Transform commands to adjust the size and shape of the neon image to fit within the boundaries of the plate (see Figure 5.26). After the transformation fits the correct dimensions, accept it.

Figure 5.25 *Paste and flip the neon image into the sidewalk image.*

Figure 5.26 *Transform the shape of the neon layer to fit in the cover-plate area.*

You can start working to make the sidewalk match the neon, appear to be taken after dark, and look as though the stones are wet. How? Well, let's look at that. First, select the layer containing the sidewalk with the plate removed (see Figure 5.27). The neon image should still be open in the background of Photoshop. If not, you will need to reopen it and then return to this image and layer.

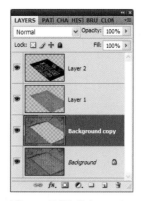

Figure 5.27 Select the sidewalk layer.

Choose Image → Adjustments → Match Color. This step will do two things for you: enable you to darken the image to make it appear as though the photo had been taken at night, and enable you to create the illusion that the stone is wet. Before playing with the sliders, look at the bottom of the Match Color dialog box, at the Image Statistics section. Set the Source to neon.jpg. The neon image will appear in the viewer to the right. Set Layer to Background and turn off the Background copy.

Blending the Photos into a New Scene

Now you can adjust the Luminance, Color Intensity, and Fade sliders. Use the settings shown in Figure 5.28 and keep an eye on the image itself.

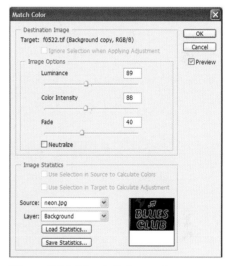

Figure 5.28 Match Color settings

You will see the image take on a blue hue, with the lighter stones embedded in the brick becoming lighter, making it appear as though the sidewalk is wet. Click OK (see Figure 5.29).

Select the Burn tool and set it to darken the Highlights:

Brush	125
Hardness	30%
Range	Highlights
Exposure	78%

Figure 5.29 The sidewalk at night

First, darken the edges of the neon layer so that the light edges blend into the dark recesses of the sidewalk (see Figure 5.30).

Figure 5.30 *Darken the edges of the neon layer.*

Next, select the sidewalk layer and look at the cracks and seams where the bricks come together. By burning these areas, you can make it appear that the seams are wetter than the stone exposed more prominently to the air. Change the Burn Range to Shadows. Run the Burn tool over these cracks, and also around the edges where the plate recesses into the sidewalk (see Figure 5.31).

The stone looks wet, but more moisture can be added. The neon is reflecting off a pool of water, at least in my brain, so that effect can be simulated with a few ripples. Select the neon layer and make an oval selection with the Elliptical Marquee tool (see Figure 5.32).

Figure 5.31 *Use the Burn tool to add water to the cracks in the stone.*

Figure 5.32 *Elliptical selection*

Open the Filters menu and choose Distort →
ZigZag. Look at Figure 5.33 and enter the settings
shown there to generate some ripples. Click OK.

Make four or more oval selections across the
surface and repeat the rippling process each time.
Alter the width of the selections to indicate variation
in the size of the raindrops hitting the surface (see
Figure 5.34).

Next we'll really make this water come to life.

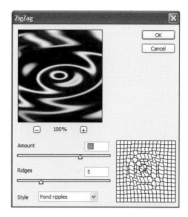

Figure 5.33 Use
*ZigZag to apply a
few ripples.*

Figure 5.34 Raindrops

Adding Liquid Transparency

Because the pool consists of water, some of the cover plate
should be seen beneath the surface. To do this, make the cover
layer visible once again and select the neon layer. Reduce the
opacity of the neon layer to 75% (see Figure 5.35).

Reducing the opacity will wash out the color of the neon
layer, but a quick adjustment of the Brightness/Contrast will
fix that. Choose Image → Adjustments → Brightness/Contrast
and change the Brightness setting to 50 and the Contrast setting to 52. Click OK.

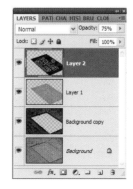

Figure 5.35 Add
*transparency to the
water.*

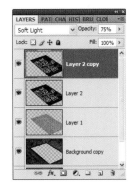

Figure 5.36
New Soft
Light layer

The neon could be a bit brighter, as could the reflections on the ripples. Duplicate the neon layer and set the blending mode to Soft Light (see Figure 5.36). Figure 5.37 shows the final image. Does it look like water to you? Did the vision stay true to that described in the beginning of this section?

This process has other possible applications. Transforming objects to conform to other molds is a good thing to know. You can conform labels to products, fit buildings to scenes where they do not belong, and so forth. Water and ripples can help you transform outdoor shots into pond reflections; you can add liquid to an image without a drop of fluid.

Figure 5.37 *Final water image*

Changing the Mood

The idea behind the next two effects is to take a photo of an area and turn it into a more sinister version of itself. I've chosen two examples: a graveyard, which is already fairly dark by nature, and a serene wood at sunset.

Because two effects will be presented here, my brain has conjured two results. The first, to be centered on the graveyard photo, is to create a world of combined texture and line art that will render a stark, gloomy version of the original photograph. The second, centered on a calm woodland path, is to re-create my version of a forest in nightmares and horror movies—a place devoid of color, warmth, and hope, where ghostly images may appear at any moment on the path before you.

Both techniques will follow the same path to their fruition, although the effects will be quite different from one another. These effects will be realized by a combination of Difference layers, adjustment layers, and a liberal application of curves. Here we will dip into the realm of the night, letting the phantoms of our imaginations show us their world: stark and cold and... dark.

We'll delve into this effect by changing the mood of an old field of tombstones into a scene from the darker side of the imagination.

From Calm to Creepy: The Graveyard

Start with the graveyard photo (see Figure 5.38); open `graveyard.jpg` from the Chapter 5 `Source Files` folder on this book's CD. Although some daylight is evident in this photo, the scene still appears bleak, with the stone faces in shadow.

To start creating the effect that I have in mind, duplicate the Background layer. Choose Image → Adjustments → Invert (see Figure 5.39).

Figure 5.38 *Graveyard at sunset*

Figure 5.39 *Graveyard inverted*

Create another copy of the Background layer. Place this new layer at the top of the layer stack and change the blending mode to Difference (see Figure 5.40). Difference is going to give us a color reversal of sorts, which can serve to achieve some very other-worldly effects. This will draw out much of the color in the sky and clouds, as well as darken the edges of the tombstones and the chapel in the background. Why is that important? Because it will give the curve some darker areas to work on, as you will see (see Figure 5.41).

Figure 5.40 Difference blending mode

Before you get to the Curves adjustment layer, create a Hue/Saturation adjustment layer at the top of the layer stack and decrease the Saturation to –90. Click OK. I realize that this setting will take most of the color away that was created before, but what I mainly wanted there wasn't the color at all, but better definition to the lines in the image.

Now create a Curves adjustment layer, as shown in Figure 5.42. This is going to increase the brightness and darkness in areas where a normal curve would not. For instance, the midtones may turn very bright while normally light areas will turn dark.

Figure 5.41 Inverted scene, more color, better definition

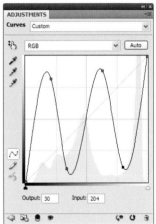

Figure 5.42 Curves adjustment

Last, take away some of the effects that the curve had on the clouds by painting in the cloud area with black, directly in the mask for the Curves adjustment layer (see Figure 5.43).

Figure 5.44 shows the final image. Compare this to the original: this effect brought even the text on the stones out of the shadows, whereas in the original photo this side of the church and headstones was in darkness.

Figure 5.43 Reduce the effect of the curves adjustment on the cloud.

Figure 5.44 *Gloomy surreal boneyard*

Darkening Another Calm Scene

Now you'll apply a similar technique, turning a serene forest image into a scene out of *The Blair Witch Project*, *The Ring* movies, or any other popular horror movie of recent years. Actually, it reminds me of the woods in the *Evil Dead* movies. Long live Ash! (Something for my fellow Deadites out there....)

To begin, open `forest.jpg` (see Figure 5.45).

Figure 5.45 *A pleasant walk in the woods*

Figure 5.46
*The Background
Copy layer settings*

Figure 5.47
*Background
Copy 2 layer settings*

As before, create two copies of the Background layer (see Figure 5.46). Invert the first (Image → Adjustments → Invert), and set the blending mode for the second to Difference. This time, reduce the fill opacity of the Difference layer to 40% (see Figure 5.47).

Figure 5.48 shows the new forest—very pretty in an odd sort of way.

Create a Hue/Saturation adjustment layer again, with nearly identical settings to those seen in the graveyard exercise (see Figure 5.49). Next, create a Curves adjustment layer at the top of the layer stack, this time using the curve shown in Figure 5.50.

The result is an image that almost appears to have been created with ink on a harsh negative (see Figure 5.51).

I can almost see a ghostly figure walking up the path toward me!

Figure 5.49 *Hue/
Saturation adjustment*

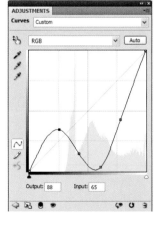

Figure 5.50
Dark-wood curve

Figure 5.48 *On our way to Happyland, via the '60s*

Figure 5.51 *Haunted woods*

Summary

Photoshop CS4 is wonderful for expanding those natural settings into otherworldly vistas, whether creating sky castles, adding water and reflections of neon on a normally dry daylight object, or turning your backyard into a thing of dread and fear. We've looked at all these aspects in this chapter, and I have a feeling you won't look at those nature photos quite the same again.

I hope you have enjoyed this little excursion into the alteration of scenic photos. This closes out the chapter on landscapes, although we are far from done working on natural images. Next you'll move on to animals—let's see what sort of right-brain mischief we can come up with in the animal kingdom.

six

Animals

At times, photos lend themselves *to the creative process simply by being what they are. Photographers are always trying to capture their subjects in the perfect light, the perfect pose, the perfect situation that conveys a mood or delivers a message. Photographers reach out with their art to invoke a response in the viewer.*

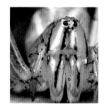

The digital artist can work with Photoshop to reinforce the link between artist/photographer and viewer. Whether the artist is going for shock value, emotion, or comfort, Photoshop can be used to enhance the mood of a photo by using textures and pigments resident in the original, or to change the mood of the message that the image conveys by combining images. This chapter takes natural elements and creatures from the world around us to demonstrate these points.

The images referenced as source files for these techniques can be found in the Chapter 6 `Source Files` *folder on this book's CD.*

Comical Critter Alteration

If you have ever purchased a greeting card or simply browsed the aisles at a gift shop, I'm sure you have seen cards with the humorous animal manipulations that have clearly been run through the Photoshop mill. Kittens and puppies in comical situations and poses can put a smile on the face of the most hardened, disgruntled card buyer. Are they cute? Most of them. Are they funny? Certainly they are. Do they sell cards for the company that distributes them? You bet they do. In turn this means a paycheck for the artist.

To open this chapter on creature manipulations, I am going to demonstrate one way in which these types of distorted, "warm-the-heart" effects can be generated. If you are already thinking about the Liquify tool, you are on the right track; that will certainly come into play for this technique. What I want to demonstrate primarily in this section is the Lens Correction filter. This was new to Photoshop CS2 and is powerful alone—and especially powerful when combined with other Photoshop processes.

The work in this section will be performed on one of those images that are too cute in their own right. Open puppy.jpg found on this book's CD (see Figure 6.1).

If you take a quick peek at Figure 6.2, you will see I've skipped a couple of processes in my description to get to this point. These are covered elsewhere in this book, so they seemed a bit redundant to rehash here. All I've done is extract the puppy from its background (see Chapter 1, "Tools for Building Your Masterpiece") and used Liquify (the Bloat tool in Chapter 2, "Techniques for Embellishing Portraits") to increase the size of the eyes and nose. The extracted puppy is placed above a layer filled with white.

Figure 6.1 A sad-eyed puppy

Figure 6.2 The puppy has been extracted and distorted with Liquify.

You will note that Figure 6.2 also has two grid lines, one vertical and one horizontal, meeting at a central point. I have created this "grid" by using the rulers to find the central point in the document. You create guides by making the ruler visible (View → Rulers) and then click-dragging with the mouse from the ruler to the document. I then moved the puppy layer so that the center of the face, or at least the center of the area I would like to expand with the Lens Correction filter, is centered in the document. This is because the Lens

Correction uses a center reference to apply corrections or, in this case, distortions. You will see what I mean momentarily.

After your puppy has been extracted, liquified, and centered, ensure that the puppy layer is selected and choose Filter → Distort → Lens Correction. The Lens Correction filter is designed to correct common lens flaws that photographers face, such as barrel and pincushion distortion, *vignetting* (my word for darkening at the corners), and chromatic aberration (color fringe on an object's edge). It is also designed to rotate or fix perspective in a photo, a common problem when the photo was taken at a slight angle or above or below the scene. In a way, this works like the familiar Transform tools, but Lens Correction is a bit easier to manipulate to dress up the photo.

A dialog box similar to the Liquify dialog box will appear with your puppy covered by a gray grid. The grid is simply to aid in correction, but this technique uses the Lens Correction filter not to correct but to alter. For instance, if you move the Remove Distortion slider to the left (negative value), a barrel effect is applied rather than reduced. I am looking for a comical or cartoonish effect for the dog, and setting the Remove Distortion slider to a positive or negative 45 value will increase the size of the face starting at the central point.

The second setting that I'm concerned with for this process is the Vertical Perspective slider in the Transform section. By moving this slider to the left, the top of the photo moves nearer the lens and the bottom farther away. A slider setting of positive or negative 100 will make the head and face appear larger, and the feet and body smaller.

Notice how the photo increases in size beyond the borders. This can be fixed as well to fit within the original frame by moving the Scale slider at the bottom of the Lens Correction dialog box to the left or by simply typing in the size percentage manually. A setting of 90% in this case reduces the size of the dog enough to bring it back within the frame. Figure 6.3 shows the Lens Correction dialog box with the settings adjusted. After you are satisfied, click OK to apply the changes to the puppy layer. Figure 6.4 shows the subject after Lens Correction has been applied.

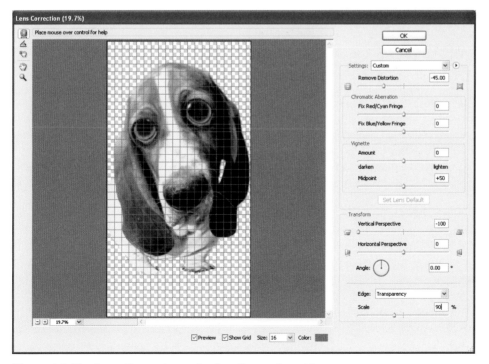

Figure 6.3 *Use Lens Correction to further distort the subject.*

Figure 6.4 Awww...

This photo is cool in its own right and is certainly one you might expect to see on a "Get Well" card. You could stop when you reach this point, or continue on and create a hand-drawn version as I will do now. This is done using steps similar to those for the plane in Chapter 8, "Going Beyond Canned Filters."

To convert the image to a painting or hand-drawn image, choose Filter → Artistic → Cutout (see Figure 6.5). This separates the primary tones in the photo into levels, sort of like a paint-by-numbers kit. For this effect, simply set Number Of Levels to 5, Edge Simplicity to 4, and Edge Fidelity to 1. Click OK.

Now that the colors have been separated, you can further enhance the hand-painted look by adding a border to the color separations. Filter → Artistic → Poster Edges works nicely here. Open the filter's dialog box and set Edge Thickness to 2, Edge Intensity to 1, and Posterization to 2, as shown in Figure 6.6. Click OK. As these filters can be stacked in the Gallery, you may want to stretch your artistic legs and experiment with these and other filter applications.

Figure 6.5 *The Cutout filter gives a "paint-by-numbers" feel to the image.*

Figure 6.6 *Separate the colors further by using the Poster Edges filter.*

Now you can duplicate the manipulated area and use blending modes (Overlay works well) or adjustment layers to enhance the color of the paint. Also, the technique used in Chapter 2, "Techniques for Embellishing Portraits," to alter the color of hair or eyes can give your pound puppy pretty blue peepers (say that three times fast!).

Figure 6.7 shows my final image.

Figure 6.7 We all just need a little love.

Attack of the Giant Bug—in 3D!

As a boy growing up in Montana in the late '60s to mid '70s before the introduction of cable television or dynamic, computer-generated special effects, I often spent my Saturday afternoons watching the weekly fare offered by one of the local television stations. Winter in Montana, especially in those days, did not allow for many outdoor activities: the temperature and snowfall would keep my brother and me indoors climbing walls, much to my mother's dismay.

Every weekend, the local television station would broadcast (at 2 o'clock precisely) some B-grade science-fiction movie or scary flick from the '50s or early '60s. My brother and I, as well as any friend that we had over at the house, would sit glued to the TV watching all manner of creatures, either diabolical or misunderstood, rampage through the streets or terrorize small communities such as we lived in. Occasionally one of these movies would be in 3D, which was always interesting to watch considering we did not have 3D glasses in central Montana at that time. When I finally did see my first 3D movie with the glasses, it was a revelation, and this genre would be a welcome comeback in the new millennium.

A couple of years ago, a good friend of mine in the industry asked whether I knew how to generate in Photoshop 3D images similar to those seen in those old movies. At that time I did not, but he piqued my interest. This technique was born from that question. Keep in mind that in order to see the effect properly you'll need to obtain a pair of standard red-and-blue 3D glasses. A simple Google search online will turn up many sites offering these items for free or relatively inexpensively. I'm including this technique to show you a unique way that you might display your art. If you do not have a pair of 3D glasses at hand, you'll have to trust me: this works!

To begin, open the image `bigbug.jpg` (see Figure 6.8).

Figure 6.8 Where does a bug like me find a little radioactivity these days?

The trick to creating a 3D effect is to separate the photo into offset reds and blue-greens. Duplicate the background layer twice and rename the first copy **Blue-Green** and the second copy **Red** (see Figure 6.9).

Because the layers need to be offset from one another, the canvas needs to be a bit larger to accommodate the offset so you don't lose the edges of the photo. Choose Image → Canvas Size and change both Width and the Height to 125% of the original size, as shown in Figure 6.10. Click OK.

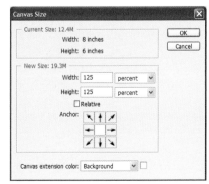

Figure 6.9 Set up the Layers panel for 3D.

Figure 6.10 Increase the canvas size.

Figure 6.11 *Use the Levels adjustment on the red channel to take the red out of the Blue-Green layer.*

Select the Blue-Green layer; then choose Image → Adjustments → Levels. You are going to "get the red out" of this layer by selecting the red channel and moving the center slider in the histogram. You may also do this manually by typing **0.10** in the center Input Levels box in this dialog box (see Figure 6.11). Turn off the Red layer if you would like to see the adjustment in action, but remember to turn it on later. Click OK to accept the adjustment.

You're almost done already. Select the Red layer and change the blending mode to Screen. Click the Move tool, and with the arrow keys, move the Blue-Green layer 5–10 taps to the right. This provides part of the offset required for the effect. Go ahead and move this layer a few taps to the left—when the Move tool is selected, you can use the arrow keys to position the layer (see Figure 6.12).

Figure 6.12 *A blending-mode change is required to make the Red layer visible.*

Now you simply need to remove the blue and green. Open the Levels dialog box for this layer and select the blue channel. Move the center slider to the left. Repeat this process with the green channel (see Figure 6.13). Click OK to accept the change.

You can see the result in Figure 6.14. If you have a pair of 3D glasses handy, the bug will appear to be residing on the glass of your monitor, giving it almost an aquarium affect. You can also use two photos of the same subject slightly offset from one another to try to further enhance the end result.

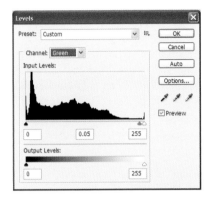

Figure 6.13 *Remove the blue and green from the Red layer with Levels.*

Figure 6.14 *My computer has a bug!*

Because you are working with a single photo rather than an offset pair, the Transform tools can be used to alter perspective on each just a bit. The human eyes are offset by an inch or so; this allows us to judge distance and see things three-dimensionally. By transforming the perspective on each layer, you can create this quality. Select the Blue-Green layer and choose Edit → Transform → Perspective. Click on the upper-left corner of the bounding box and move it down slightly (see Figure 6.15). Repeat this process with the Red layer, but move the upper-right corner of the bounding box.

Figure 6.15 *Adjust perspective on each layer a bit to mimic how our eyes see the world.*

If the image is too dark, which it may well be after you put on a pair of 3D glasses, you can simply apply a standard Brightness/Contrast adjustment layer and edit accordingly. In this instance, increase the Brightness to 20 and the Contrast to 15 (see Figures 6.16 and 6.17).

After the transformation is complete, furthering the offset to duplicate how our eyes see the world, you can crop the image as you like. The final shot appears in Figure 6.18.

I expect to see 3D posters appearing for sale at the county fair in the near future!

Figure 6.16 *A slight Brightness/Contrast adjustment*

Figure 6.17 *All layers in place*

Figure 6.18 *A science experiment gone horribly awry!*

Creature out of Place

Photographs themselves often inspire a digital artist to create. In the first edition of this book, I wrapped a snake around a woman to demonstrate how one can relatively easily take a subject from one photo and place it in a totally different environment. That environment need not be something desirable or comical, but can be quite undesirable for the subject in the photo. Dark artists manipulate photography in this manner frequently; others do this just for fun.

Either way, this technique demonstrates two processes: how to take a subject from one photo and put it in another (as you've seen with the apple in Chapter 1), and how to change the mood of a piece by using color and stark lighting/shadows. This will also demonstrate that even though an image appears as though it is a little rough in the midst of the process, it can occasionally be salvaged and used anyway.

The two images used in this section are `yell.jpg` and `spider.jpg`. Please have them open and ready.

Select the image `yell.jpg` (see Figure 6.19). I envision the final image in my mind's eye on a dark or black background. For this reason, you should extract the subject from his surroundings. The edges are well defined and there is no hair to deal with, so this extraction should go fairly smoothly. Go through the process you learned in Chapter 1 and extract the man from the background, placing him in his own layer. See Figure 6.20.

Figure 6.20 Extract the man from his natural habitat.

Figure 6.19 I'm telling ya, there's a huge spider here somewhere!

Now create a new layer, fill it with black, and move it beneath the man layer. Another point to consider is that the man's head is almost touching the top edge of the photo. I envision the spider resting on top of the man's head, so the canvas size will need to be increased. Choose Image → Canvas Size and increase the Height to 200%. Refill the black layer so that the entire backdrop is black (see Figure 6.21). The extracted man will be in the middle of the image, so select the Move tool, and holding down the Shift key, tap the Down arrow until the man is at the bottom of the canvas. If it isn't already, fill the entire background image with black (see Figure 6.22).

Switch over to the image `spider.jpg` (see Figure 6.23). This guy (or gal; I've never been able to tell with spiders) is to be removed from its background also and pasted into the other image. Using the Pen tool and, following the techniques explained in Chapter 1, extract the spider from the background. Don't worry about the hairs… go ahead and make your selection without them (see Figure 6.24).

Figure 6.21 Layers-panel pecking order thus far

Figure 6.23 Cousin to the 3D radioactive spider

Figure 6.22 An expanded canvas   *Figure 6.24 Spider searching for a new home*

After the spider has been removed from its background, copy and paste it into a new layer in the original image. Move the spider so that it is just above the man's head (see Figure 6.25).

Now the spider needs to shed some weight. Use the Transform tools to manipulate it so that it appears to be standing on the man's head (see Figure 6.26).

You will want the forelegs to extend over the crown of the man's skull. Create a mask on the head layer (Figure 6.27) and paint with black over the area where the forelegs are. To ensure you are getting the correct areas covered with the paint, reduce the opacity of the head layer until the painting is done. You may also generate a selection in the shape of the spider to ensure the paint stays within the lines (see Figure 6.28).

Figure 6.26 Use the Transform tools to conform the spider's size and shape to fit on top of the man's head.

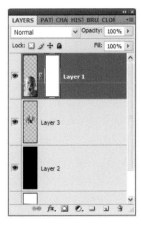

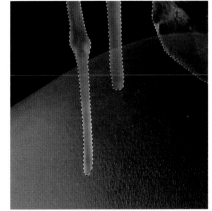

Figure 6.25 It's hard to find a good parking spot these days.

Figure 6.27 Add a mask to the head.

Figure 6.28 Reveal the forelegs.

To make the spider appear at home in its new habitat, the light needs to hit the spider at the same angle as it is reflecting on the man's face. You can exemplify this illusion by using the Burn tool to create shadows beneath the spider legs on the man's head. Select the man's head layer. Click the Burn tool, and using a semi-feathered brush with the Range set to Midtones and Exposure to 50% (see Figure 6.29), darken regions beneath the legs to make it appear as though shadows from the legs are on the scalp. Duplicate the spider layer and set the blending mode for the new layer to Overlay. This will add some color to the spider and help those edges a bit (see Figure 6.30).

This is turning into an emotional piece: I certainly would not want to be in this man's situation without a very large newspaper! You can now use color and stark contrasts to enhance the electric emotion this man must be feeling.

Figure 6.29 Burning the shadows

Figure 6.30 A new home for Charlotte

First, merge all layers into a single layer, as shown in Figure 6.31. You're going to use our old friend Apply Image to enhance the contrasts in this image. Choose Image → Apply Image and set the source to yell.jpg. See Figure 6.32 for the exact settings; the main one to be concerned with is Blending. Ensure that this is changed to Hard Mix.

Figure 6.31 Merge them all together.

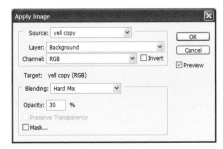

Figure 6.32 Apply Image revisited

If you are unhappy with how the legs turned out (there was a bit of clipping that occurred during the paths extraction), simply trim that portion of the image away. Figure 6.33 shows the end result. Just by that Apply Image adjustment, the emotion of this piece is changed dramatically, as is the artistic style. To repeat myself once again, often just a simple change in blending mode or filter application or adjustment-layer application can have a dramatic effect on your digital art. I encourage you to experiment with other blending modes and settings you've seen throughout the book to see how far you can take this!

Crossbreeding Species: Human Lioness

It is said that some people resemble their pets and vice versa. Often people choose pets that remind them of themselves both physically and in their nature. There seem to be factors differentiating "cat people" and "dog people." Most pet owners can be divided into one of these two categories.

In Photoshop, you can take this to the limit and beyond—not simply by creating a resemblance, but by actually merging the characteristics of two creatures into a single image, generating an entirely new species. For this

Figure 6.33 Honey, I found your pet!

piece I envision a combination of human and feline characteristics. Although it sounds as though this could be complicated to pull off, that isn't the case at all. Using some of the masking techniques already learned (you are probably pretty well versed in masks by now), combining a lion with a person will be a cakewalk.

Although I'm usually working until the wee hours of the morning, I try to watch *Late Night with Conan O'Brien* when I can. The humor is often rather base, but I'm a little off in my sense of humor. One bit on the show combines photos of people to see what their children would look like. The following example is an offshoot of that.

Begin with two images from this book's CD: `leo.jpg` and `intense.jpg` (see Figures 6.34 and 6.35). Make a copy of the image of the woman and paste it into a new layer in the lion document. Reduce the opacity of the woman layer to 60%; this way, you can see the lion beneath to line up the images in the next step (see Figure 6.36).

Figure 6.34 *King of the jungle*

Figure 6.35 *Queen of the business world*

Figure 6.36 *Preparing layers for the merge*

Choose Edit → Transform → Scale and increase the size of the woman's face so that her eyes overlay those of the lion. Also position the lips so that the woman's lower lip extends below the pleat in the lion's upper lip, below its nose (see Figure 6.37). When everything is in its proper place, accept the transformation.

It's time to meld the two faces with a mask. Increase the Opacity of the face layer to 100%. Create a layer mask for the woman's face layer (see Figure 6.38). Select the Paintbrush tool and set black as the foreground color.

Using a fairly large, round, feathered brush, begin painting in the mask to hide portions of the woman's face, such as the nose, cheeks, and so forth. Leave her lower lip visible, as well as her eyes and strands of hair hanging down on the left side of the image (see Figure 6.39). Continue working on the mask with black paint until most of her face is hidden, leaving only the eyes, eyebrows, and the lower lip visible (see Figure 6.40).

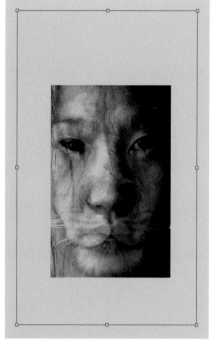

Figure 6.38 Create a mask for the woman's face.

Figure 6.37 Match facial features between the two photos.

Figure 6.39 Hide portions of the woman, revealing the cat beneath.

Figure 6.40 The lioness revealed

For a few final touches, add some color to the irises as you did in the coloring exercises in Chapter 2. I love emerald on cats, so I've applied green to the eyes here (see Figure 6.41). Also add some color to the lips.

Last, increase the richness of the color of the overall image. You can do this with Apply Image (Image → Apply Image). First, merge the layers together. Use this image as the source and set the blending mode to Overlay. Adjust the opacity slider until you are happy with the tone.

Figure 6.42 shows the final lioness photo. I love the color of this piece, as well as the seamless melding of facial features from both photographs for a combined whole.

Figure 6.41 *Add color to the eyes.*

Figure 6.42 *The lioness realized*

Crossbreeding Species 2: Pegasus

Following the theme of fanciful creature creation, let's delve into one more area of popularity: creatures of myth. I've long been a fan of fantasy novels. If I feel the need to unwind and get away from the computer for a while, you will find me either working in my garden or yard, or simply sitting for hours with my nose buried in a swords-and-sorcery paperback. (If you are into that sort of thing, I strongly suggest you check out the works of one of my favorite authors, R.A. Salvatore, creator of the dark elf hero Drizzt Do'Urden. Now there is time well spent!)

Back to the technique. My thought for this piece is to create a Pegasus, one of the more noble and intelligent creatures from mythology, in a scene that could be in your neighbor's field on a cool January morning.

Open the images `horse2.jpg` and `swan.jpg` (see Figures 6.43 and 6.44).

Figure 6.43 *Grazing on a summer's morn*

Figure 6.44 *Hey, buddy... tell me again. Why didn't we go south this year?*

Once again, masks will come into play to help realize the vision. First, copy the swan photo and paste it into a new layer in the horse document (see Figure 6.45). Reduce the

opacity of the swan layer so the layer beneath can be used as a reference. Select the Move tool and position the swan photo so that the swan on the left is over the horse in such a way that the wings appear as if they could be protruding from either animal. Aim for the withers (top of the front shoulder) on the horse for the wing placement (see Figure 6.46).

You may now create a mask for the swan layer and hide everything with the exception of the wings. Note that you will need to remove the neck of the swan from the photo as well, which will leave a gap between the wings (see Figure 6.47).

Figure 6.45 *Place both images in the same document.*

Figure 6.46 *Position the trailing swan above the horse.*

Figure 6.47 *Mask away the swans, leaving only the wings.*

Paint with white in the mask over the neck again, revealing it. I'm having you reveal it again so you may use the Clone tool to replace the neck in this layer with wings instead. Otherwise, you will be left with a huge gap, and that just won't do.

Click the Clone tool and verify the layer mask is not selected. My settings are shown in Figure 6.48. All I'm doing is sampling portions of the swan's wing next to the neck and stamping it over the neck. Repeat the process until the neck disappears, leaving only feathers. Work as carefully as possible so that the feathers in this area match the direction and size of those in the rest of the wing. Figure 6.49 shows the Layers panel at this stage of the game.

Figure 6.48 Clone-tool settings

The current state of the image is shown in Figure 6.50. At this point, you have a sepia horse and background, and bright bluish-white feathery wings protruding from the back of the sepia horse. Its current state is not very realistic, even for a mythical photograph. Some adjustment will need to be made. Duplicate the Background layer (see Figure 6.51). Can you guess where I'm going next?

Figure 6.49 Layers-panel progress check

Figure 6.50 The wings are in place, but the ambient colors don't yet match.

That's right; you guessed it. Match Color is going to help you match the color of the horse layer to that of the wings. You can do it the other way around if you so choose, matching the wings to the ambient light of the horse layer, but in the beginning of this exercise I mentioned seeing the Pegasus in a field in winter. Click on the horse layer in the Layers panel.

Figure 6.51 Set up the Layers panel for a color change.

Figure 6.52 shows my Match Color settings. The thing to keep in mind in this instance is the source. You want the horse layer to match the color of the swan layer, so by sending the Source in Match Color to the swan photo, the horse layer will take on those color characteristics. You may also adjust the Luminance, Color Intensity, and Fade settings to taste until you get a good blend. Keep an eye on your image while making these adjustments until you are happy with the result. My final shot of a Pegasus grazing in a midwinter field is shown in Figure 6.53.

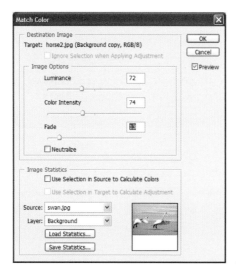

Figure 6.52 Match color between images.

Figure 6.53 I took a walk on a winter morn, and strange things did I see....

Summary

We covered some fairly drastic manipulation effects in this chapter, from the ever-popular Liquify tool to some horrific blending of one creature into another photo, and we even delved into the realm of faux 3D. Apply Image was there to aid in the process, and Photoshop techniques we've seen and practiced before helped achieve some definite right-brained images.

I hope you have enjoyed this chapter on creature manipulations. As always, the creatures you make and the art you create are limited only by your understanding of the tools, their application, and your imagination. Let your imagination soar and see what materializes on the screen.

Next on the agenda: we'll look at digital manipulations for advertising, as well as some practical blending and sharpening, although in ways you may not have seen before. I'm all about stretching the boundaries… both yours and those of the software. Always stretch before the workout!

seven

Digital Alterations and Manipulations

When I was younger, everything *art-related
fell into two general categories: Cool or Dumb. I didn't understand the
spirit behind the art. I'd see a broken cup glued to a wall and, rather than
appreciate anything the artist may have been trying to convey, I'd chuck it
into the latter category (I'm still not sure about that piece). Anything by
Boris Vallejo—airbrushed, seminude women with giant winged reptiles—
was Good Art, and anything else was decidedly Lame, Dumb, and so on
and so forth.*

I still love Boris (www.imaginistix.com) *but now also appreciate other
forms of artistic expression. I never used to understand stationary objects
or common household items taking prominence in photographic art, but
now I can see that they play a vital role in advertising (yes, even
advertising can be considered an art form), illustrating retro styles and
making simple statements about our lives in the new millennium.
Displaying a product to render it appealing isn't an easy process; an artist
needs that right-brain imagination.*

*This chapter delves into three interesting areas: advertising, object
photos used as artistic renderings, and even a simple object enhanced by
using its own characteristics as a form of expression. There are a couple
of pretty standard takes and a couple that are possible only because
Photoshop is in the darkroom. Let's get into it, shall we?*

*The images referenced as source files for these techniques can be
found in the Chapter 7* Source Files *folder on this book's CD.*

Digital Woman

As I mentioned, advertising is an art form—or at least artistic elements are used in the advertising medium. This art form is called *graphic arts*, after all. To reflect that point, this exercise will show one way to build an ad from an idea, by using Photoshop, your own gray matter, and a whole lot of imagination.

The premise is fairly direct: create a unique advertising piece reflecting people and the digital world. This image should use a logo prominently. To ensure that the logo sticks out, you can use it repetitively (or in more than one instance). The ad should not only display the logo but should also encapsulate the company slogan.

To realize this technique, you will require a logo and a face. You will capture a photo by using a converted text layer and combinations of masks, blending-mode changes, and colorizing techniques to complete the final image.

Beginning the Process

To start the ad, you will first create a digital image. I can hear it already... "Wait a minute, Al; aren't we already working with digital images?" Sure, we are, but that isn't really what I have in mind. How about if the main character consisted of ones and zeros, literally? It's worth a try.

Open the image `glasses.jpg` (see Figure 7.1) on this book's CD-ROM. This photo has elements that I think will fit nicely in the final image, in particular the reflections on the large lenses. You'll soon see what I have in mind, but first let's really make this woman digital.

Now that the primary image is open, it is time to set up the Layers panel. Create a new layer just above the Background layer and fill it with black. Next, duplicate the Background layer and place it above the black layer. Rename the new copy of the woman **Glasses-1**, and move the layer to the left about one-third the width of the image. This will give some space on the right for additional ad copy after the primary image is complete (see Figure 7.2).

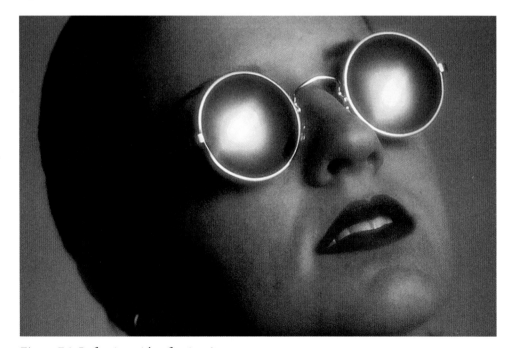

Figure 7.1 Reflective with reflections?

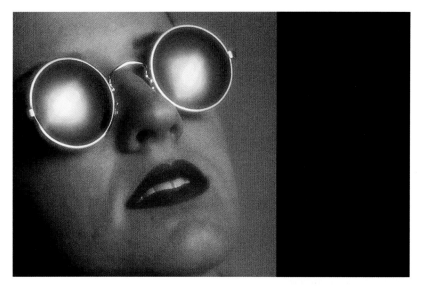

Figure 7.2 Leave space for the ad text.

You need a layer consisting of ones and zeros to use in the image conversion, so select the Vertical Type tool. On the Options bar, set the font to Arial Black, Regular, 12 pts, Top Justify, and set the font color to white. Starting in the upper-right corner of the face layer (you need not cover the black portion of the image), make four columns of ones and zeros, typed randomly (see Figure 7.3). Rasterize and duplicate the Type layer, move the new layer to the left to create four more columns, and merge those layers to create an eight-column layer. Repeat the process until the entire face is covered (see Figure 7.4). Rename the final merged-character layer **Numbers**.

⌘/Ctrl-click the Numbers layer to select all of the type. Select the Glasses-1 layer and copy it (⌘/Ctrl+C). Paste the pixel information into a new layer; then name the layer **Face-Numbers**. Move the layer over the original face until the numbers vanish. Duplicate the layer and set the blending mode for the new layer to Overlay (see Figure 7.5).

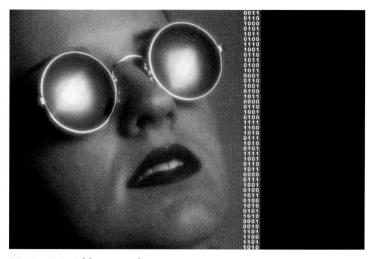

Figure 7.3 Add ones and zeros.

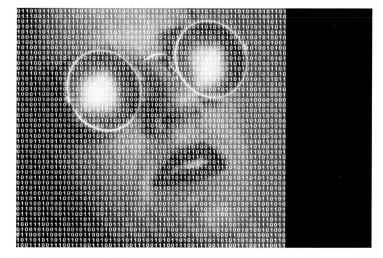

Figure 7.4 Digitized

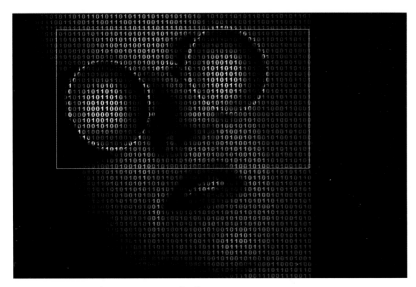

Figure 7.5 Numbers construct the face.

Return to the Glasses-1 layer. My thought was to use the reflections on the glasses to display a glowing logo, which is the primary reason this photo was so appealing to me. To do that, the lenses need to be visible in their entirety while the rest of the face remains digitized. You guessed it: a mask is about to come into play.

Create a layer mask for the Glasses-1 layer and fill it with black. Set white as the foreground color and, using the Paintbrush tool, paint over the lens areas in the mask.

The process just applied needs to be reversed for the Face-Numbers layers. In other words, the numbers need to be hidden from the lenses but revealed on the face so that the numeric construct is still visible. Create a mask for each Face-Numbers layer and fill the mask with white. Paint over the lenses with black in the masks, and also reveal the wire frame around the lenses, as shown in Figure 7.6.

The numbers bordering the face aren't needed either, so continue to paint in the Face-Numbers layers' masks and hide the characters that do not compose the face. You may also opt to recolor the lenses of the glasses: use the Color blending-mode technique shown in Chapter 2, "Techniques for Embellishing Portraits." Figure 7.7 shows the result.

Figure 7.6 Hide the numbers in the logo area.

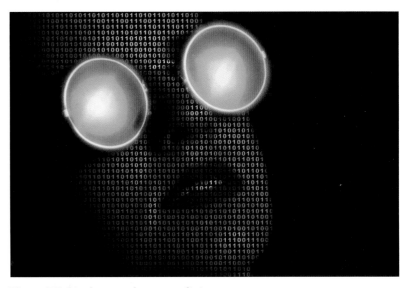

Figure 7.7 Mask away the excess digits.

Adding the Logo

Now for the logo. In considering the theme of this exercise, I worked in reverse: I knew the technique that I wanted to demonstrate before I had the product in mind. The image effect you're creating here suggests something digital and somewhat futuristic, so a computer company would be a perfect fit. So what sort of logo would work for a computer company? What would be unique but easily associated with computers? After a bit of thought, I decided on the nearly universal On button icon. Most PCs and Macs have it embedded in the face of the button.

In the real world, of course, you'd be working with an established company, and they would usually supply their logo and product information for your design.

Let's get to the logo placement. Open the image power button.jpg (see Figure 7.8). The logo needs to be transferred to the face image. Here's the process:

1. Use the Elliptical Marquee tool to select the glowing logo and the glowing circle around the On button.
2. Copy the logo to the clipboard (⌘/Ctrl+C).
3. Paste the logo into the digital face image at the top of the layer stack.
4. With the Transform tools, conform the logo into one of the lenses.
5. Duplicate the Logo layer and move this instance of the logo to the other lens.
6. Merge the two Logo layers.

After all those steps, the logos should appear on the digital face image, as shown in Figure 7.9.

Figure 7.8 *A PC On button*

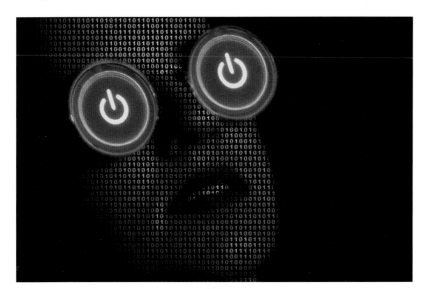

Figure 7.9 *The glowing logo is reflected on the glasses.*

Create a mask for the Logo layer. The idea is to reveal some of the reflection seen on the original lenses but to still retain the logo. Select a median gray foreground color, and paint in the mask over the center of the lenses. A brush size that covers most of the lens would work perfectly in this instance.

If you retained the glowing ring around the button when it was copied to the face image, you followed the instructions correctly. However, it might look cooler if the glowing ring were turned to metal to appear to be new frames for the lenses. How do you accomplish that?

It isn't as hard as it may sound, really. The reflections are already present in the lights; take the color away, and you should have a nice metallic frame. Create a new layer at the top of the layer stack, and set the blending mode for the new layer to Color. You should already have gray set as the foreground color, so reduce the size of the paintbrush to compensate for the width of the frame. Then just paint away the color on the frame.

To enhance the reflections, select the Dodge tool and apply it to taste on the lower-right and upper-left quadrants of the logo rings. You may also need to do this to the actual Logo layer to enhance the effect, as shown in Figure 7.10.

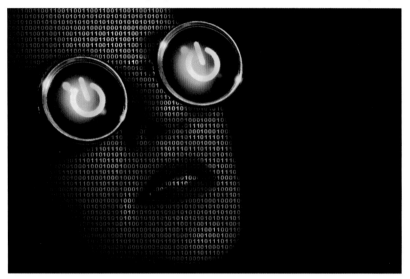

Figure 7.10 Create metallic highlights.

In the final image, I've simply added another instance of the logo, a company slogan, and information (see Figure 7.11). Something to think about when creating ad pieces (as I've tried to reflect here) is how to tie the text to the image or vice versa—for instance, the wistful look on the digital woman paired with the "Wishful Thinking" statement in the text.

This lesson did some fairly heavy image alteration to achieve a goal. There are times when heavy manipulation isn't required to generate an emotive work. Let's explore this thought in the next portion and create a final production image using simple objects and minimal manipulation.

Figure 7.11 The complete advertisement

Common Images in Art

Most photographic art does not use or require a lot of digital manipulation to inspire, to evoke, or to appeal. For this piece, you will simply apply two similar images to a background to reflect a theme.

I was a thespian in my high-school days (an actor, to those unfamiliar with the term). The Comedy and Tragedy masks were commonplace on the stage and in posters we created to advertise upcoming plays. In this section, you will create such an image by placing the masks of Comedy and Tragedy on a simple background. The process for realizing this will be a piece of cake, and with some help from Photoshop you can complete a professional-looking poster in very little time.

To start, open the image `roughBG.jpg` (see Figure 7.12) to serve as the background.

The background looks pretty good as it sits, but some shadow could be added to imply a border and take the emphasis away from the background in the final image. This is done easily with a quick layer style. Duplicate the Background layer, open the Layer Style dialog box, and select Inner Glow. Enter the following settings for the glow:

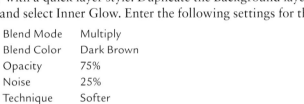

Blend Mode	Multiply
Blend Color	Dark Brown
Opacity	75%
Noise	25%
Technique	Softer
Source	Edge
Choke	0%
Size	220%

Don't worry about any of the other settings; just click OK. This will darken the border of the background gradually, as shown in Figure 7.13.

Figure 7.12 *Background for the poster*

Figure 7.13 *Darken the border.*

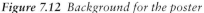

Open the image `tragedy.jpg` (see Figure 7.14). For this project, you can omit the extensive extraction described for previous exercises, because the background is a solid color and the mask is clearly defined. Use the Magic Wand to select the areas of white (press the Add To Selection button on the Options bar), select Inverse, choose Select → Contract → 2 px, and copy and paste the mask into the background image. Use the Transform tools to reduce the size of the mask if you need to, and then move it to the right side of the background until only half of the face is showing (see Figure 7.15).

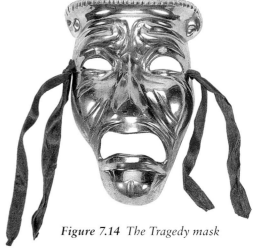

Figure 7.14 The Tragedy mask

Make the mask appear to float above the background by applying a drop shadow. Use the following settings for the shadow:

Blend Mode	Multiply
Opacity	50%
Angle	50° (with Global Light turned off)
Distance	385 px
Spread	0
Size	100 px

Figure 7.15 The mask finds a new home.

The edges of the mask could be darkened as well, just as the Background was. With the Layer Style dialog box still open, select Inner Glow from the left side, and apply the same settings as with the Background. After you enter the settings, click OK.

To enhance the mask in both tone and reflection, create a copy of the mask layer, and change the blending mode to Soft Light. Delete the applied styles for this layer.

The mask appears a bit grainy, but you don't really want to blur the primary Mask layer. Instead, a blur applied to the Soft Light layer will help clean up the graininess. ⌘/Ctrl-click a Mask layer, and run a Gaussian blur on the Soft Light layer (see Figure 7.16).

Figure 7.16 Blurring the grain

Now open the image comedy.jpg, which is the Comedy mask image. Repeat the entire process done to the other mask, with the exception of the placement on the background. Instead, angle this mask as shown in Figure 7.17; repeat all other processes done to the Tragedy mask on this mask also.

To finalize the image, you only need to darken the shadows a bit and lighten the highlights. To do so, create a Curves adjustment layer; use the settings shown in Figure 7.18.

Figure 7.19 shows the final image. The process was painless and short, yet the result looks professional.

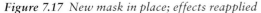

Figure 7.17 *New mask in place; effects reapplied*

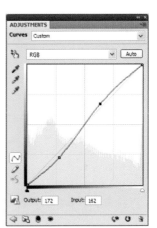

Figure 7.18 *Curves adjustment*

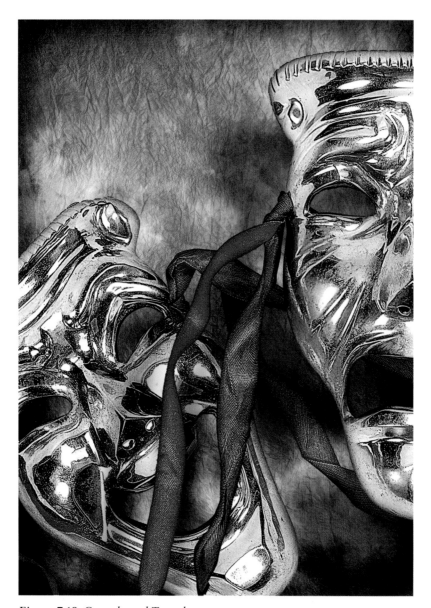

Figure 7.19 Comedy and Tragedy poster

Enhanced Close-up: Macro Art

Macro art or *macro photography* uses high-definition close-ups, showing us details that require extreme magnification to be revealed. Generally these shots require high-resolution equipment and a very steady hand. (The latter is something I've never had.) As you have seen in previous chapters, Photoshop has the tools to help generate high-definition images from pretty standard photographs. This project will bring out the richly patterned structure of a delicate flower.

 Open the image `flowers.jpg` (see Figure 7.20).

Figure 7.20 *Delicate petals*

First, enhance the image with the High Pass filter. Here's the process I use:
1. Duplicate the Background layer twice.
2. Change the blending mode for the top layer to Overlay (see Figure 7.21).
3. Choose Filter → Other → High Pass. Set the Radius for the filter to 15 pixels (see Figure 7.22).

Note that the actual veins in the petals begin to appear as you adjust the slider. When you have a good contrast, click OK. To further enhance the effect, duplicate the High Pass layer and set the blending mode to Soft Light (see Figure 7.23). The enhanced image is shown in Figure 7.24.

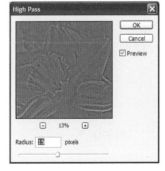

Figure 7.21 *Duplicate the Background layer twice; set the blending mode to Overlay.*

Figure 7.22 *Apply the High Pass filter trick.*

Figure 7.23 *Further enhance the image by duplicating the High Pass layer and setting the blending mode to Soft Light.*

Figure 7.24 A well-defined floral arrangement

I'm not going to play with this much, other than to add masks to all layers except the background. In photos such as this, the focus is usually on a single flower, while the rest of the arrangement and the background are softened. Creating a layer mask for each of the top three layers and drawing a white-to-black radial gradient in each with the primary flower as the center of the gradient will allow it to retain its definition while the rest of the image slowly blurs. Figure 7.25 demonstrates what the Layers panel should look like when all three masks are securely in place. Figure 7.26 shows the enhanced photo.

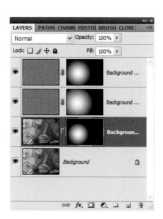

Figure 7.25 Layer masks in place

Figure 7.26 From distinct focus to soft focus

The sharpening technique works wonders on metal as well. Figures 7.27 and 7.28 show the effect on a piece of hand-tooled metal. Keep in mind that to make the effect a bit more subtle, changing the blending mode for the High Pass layers from Overlay to Soft Light and/ or reducing the opacities of those layers will allow you to control the amount of sharpening on the object or subject. In these two examples, I have not included the layer masks.

Figure 7.27 Soft, hand-tooled metal

Figure 7.28 Drastically enhanced

I'm including the following two figures as a reminder that not all sharpening is good sharpening! Figure 7.29 shows a pair of already-grumpy eyes. Bad day at work, perhaps? Figure 7.30 is the result after having applied this sharpening technique. The pores, the stray hairs, the blemishes, the freckles—everything people generally wants to correct in their photos—are brought forth with less-than-flattering results!

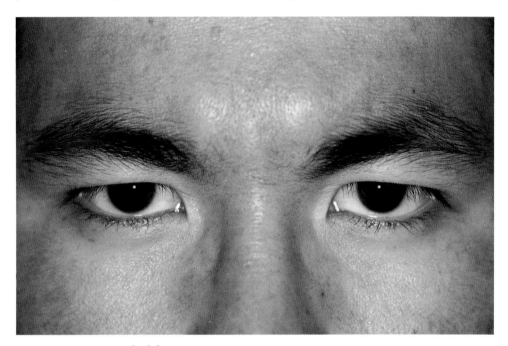

Figure 7.29 *Having a bad day*

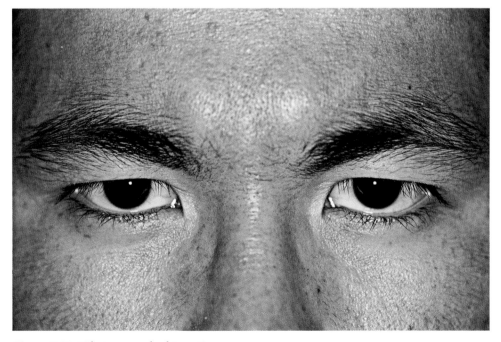

Figure 7.30 *What are you looking at?*

Summary

Whether you are generating art for an advertising campaign, creating posters for a local art show, or simply enhancing personal photographs, the tools at your disposal in Photoshop CS4 can enhance your end product a hundredfold. All it takes is a vision, some degree of direction, experience with the software, and a dash of imagination. The car will get you there once you have a route in mind and once you know how to drive. Don't forget to fuel up and check the tires!

In Chapter 8 we will work on altering photographs of a more personal nature and work to imitate art in real life. Whether your interest is in sketching, painting, or a combination of both, you'll be able to tackle these with the ease of an art-school graduate.

eight

Going Beyond Canned Filters

Filters are one of the first *features that a new Photoshop user typically starts with. They spark interest in the software, providing instant gratification with just a few clicks. You don't need to know the theory behind a filter in order to apply it to an image. The drawback to using filters is that no matter how cool an image may look after a particular filter is applied, other Photoshop users will notice the "canned" filter in an instant. Many is the time I've been asked to critique someone's "masterpiece," only to see that that person applied one or two filters and sent it out to the digital world to stun the masses. The masses, especially those who use Photoshop on a regular basis, are usually left markedly "unstunned."*

The key to using filters is to know when and where to apply one (and which one to apply) to an image that incorporates other features and tools in the program. Filters are spices; they are not the meal. Use them sparingly if you can; you should always strive to let the camera and the setup do most of the work when possible. This chapter shows several ways to make your photos appear aged, drawn, painted, and otherwise manipulated without using the Filters menu exclusively. I think you will find that the end results not only have a greater realism but are also far more satisfying.

The images referenced as source files for these techniques can be found in the Chapter 8 Source Files *folder on this book's CD.*

Retro Photo: Aging

Photoshop is not only a photo-correction tool, but as you have seen in previous chapters, it is also a great program for manipulation and the realization of digital art. The concept for this section is to take a perfectly good photograph that could have been shot yesterday and age it 60 years, complete with damage to the paper.

 Open the image dancers.jpg (see Figure 8.1) found on this book's CD. This photo could certainly be a period capture; the clothing styles are certainly not something you would expect to see being worn by the average Joe and Jane.

In the Layers panel, duplicate the Background layer. Rename the new layer **Aged**. Create a duplicate for this layer also, but turn off the visibility of the layer (Aged Copy). You will return to it soon, but first you need to do a few things to the Aged layer. Shut off the Background layer. With the Aged layer selected, choose Image → Adjustments → Desaturate, and remove all the color from the Aged layer (see Figure 8.2).

Figure 8.1 A night of romance

Figure 8.2 Setting up the Layers panel

This layer will provide the foundation for the aging process. Create a Brightness/Contrast adjustment layer just above the Aged layer but beneath the Aged Copy layer. Leave the Brightness slider alone, but increase the contrast to 25 and click OK.

One problem with a lot of old photographs is the quality of the camera or film available at the time. Graininess was a definite problem, so adding some will enhance the aged look of this piece. Select the Aged layer and choose Filter → Noise → Add Noise. In the Add Noise dialog box, set the Amount to 8% and the Distribution to Gaussian, and select Monochromatic at the bottom (see Figure 8.3). Click OK.

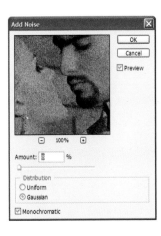

Figure 8.3 Add Noise filter in action

If you apply the Add Noise filter with Monochromatic unchecked, the filter will change the color of some pixels. With Monochromatic checked, the filter affects only the tonal elements of the image or layer, leaving the colors alone.

Create a new Hue/Saturation adjustment layer above the Brightness/Contrast adjustment layer. This layer will give the black-and-white layer beneath it a sepia tone. Most photo-aging techniques stop there, but this technique will allow some original color to be retained.

With the Hue/Saturation dialog box open, move the sliders (or type in the settings manually) as follows:

Colorize (lower-right corner)	Checked
Hue	30
Saturation	20
Lightness	0

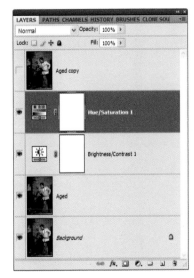

Figure 8.4 State of the Layers panel—progress check

Click OK to apply the settings. The Layers panel at this point will look like Figure 8.4.

I mentioned that some of the original color will be retained, and the Aged Copy layer will be the medium used for that color. Some manipulation of the pixels needs to take place to combine the color of this layer with the sepia from the layers beneath. You might think that a simple blending-mode change or opacity reduction will give the desired effect, but this technique is a bit more involved than that.

Select the Aged Copy layer and turn the visibility back on. Change the blending mode to Overlay and reduce the opacity to 50%. Many old photos were originally black-and-white or sepia-toned and later colored by hand. You are going to use this layer to give the photo that hand-colored effect while retaining the sepia in other areas of the picture.

Choose Select → Color Range. The default selection (indicated by white in the viewer window) should grab the shadowed areas of the image. If not, use the Eyedropper to sample the dark areas, and move the Fuzziness slider to 200. Click OK.

Figure 8.5 *Layer after shadow deletion*

With the selection active, press the Delete key. If you hold down the Option/Alt key and click the eye icon next to the layer, all other layers will become invisible and you will see the state of the current layer (see Figure 8.5). The dark areas will have been wiped away, leaving only faint colored pixels in the areas of brick, skin, and clothing. Option/Alt-click the eye icon again to turn all the layers back on.

There still seems to be a bit too much color in the overall image, so choose Select → Color Range again. This time, select Midtones from the Select menu at the top of the Color Range dialog box and click OK. Choose Layer → New → Layer Via Cut. Reduce the opacity of the new layer to 35–40%. Figure 8.6 shows the image thus far. The overall tonal effect is sepia, with just a hint of color left in the costumes and on the dancers. Trust me; it is there. If you would like a bit more color, just increase the opacity of the layer.

Figure 8.6 *Remove a few more pixels.*

With the image appropriately colored for age, you may now simulate damage to the photo produced by years of storage in a box. Normal wear and tear produces scratching; moisture can bubble or blemish the photo as well as produce mold and age spots. Photoshop can do this too, or at least give the illusion of such.

Create a new layer above the Aged Copy layer; name the new layer **Clouds**. Press the D key to reset the swatches to Black (foreground) and White (background); then choose Filter → Render → Clouds. The new layer will be filled with random areas of black, white, and gray merging in a cotton-candy pattern of gradual fluffiness. Okay, how else would you describe it?

Choose Filter → Brush Strokes → Sprayed Strokes. Set the following options:

Stroke Length	0
Spray Radius	25
Stroke Direction	Left Diagonal

Click OK. Now choose Image → Adjustments → Brightness/Contrast. Set the following options:

Brightness	75
Contrast	100

Figure 8.7 Using clouds to add color

Click OK. Change the blending mode of the Clouds layer to Multiply.

This layer can also be used to add color to the photo. Choose Image → Adjustments → Hue/Saturation, and set the options as follows. Ensure Colorize is checked. When you've finished, click OK (see Figure 8.7).

Hue	25
Saturation	25
Lightness	+20

Duplicate the Clouds layer and change the blending mode to Screen and the opacity to 20%. This will lighten the image somewhat.

It may be a good idea to save your work thus far. You can either save the image as a .psd file to retain the layers, or simply open the History panel and create a new snapshot. You can return to this state of the image at any time by selecting the snapshot in the History panel. Your image should look like Figure 8.8 at this point.

Figure 8.8 Aged, damaged, and washed out

Creating Surface Cracks

I had you save a snapshot at this point because you're going to merge all the layers with the exception of the original background. Turn off the Background layer. Open the Layers menu, and near the bottom of the menu, select Merge Visible. Duplicate this layer and name the copies **Aged-01** and **Aged-02** (see Figure 8.9).

A few more blemishes can be added in the form of cracking or peeling. To do this, create a new layer named **Cracks**, and run the Clouds filter on this layer also (Filter → Render → Clouds). Figure 8.10 shows the Layers panel.

The Clouds filter generates patterns by using soft variations between the foreground and background colors. To generate a more emphasized cloud pattern, hold down Option/ Alt as you choose Filter → Render → Clouds. When you apply the Clouds filter, the image data on the active layer is replaced. (Pixels are added on layers that have no image data.)

Open the Filters menu again, this time choosing Texture → Craquelure. This filter reproduces the effect of cracks on a plaster surface. Apply the following settings in the Craquelure dialog box:

Crack Spacing	90
Crack Depth	8
Crack Brightness	8

Click OK. Choose Image → Adjustments → Brightness/Contrast, and increase the Brightness of the layer to +75 and the Contrast to +100. Click OK.

You will not need the white in the Cracks layer, so choose Select → Color Range, and select the white portions of the layer with the Eyedropper (see Figure 8.11). Click OK, and press the Delete key to wipe away the white pixels. Deselect.

Figure 8.9 Current state of the layers

Figure 8.10 Working with clouds

Figure 8.11 Select white and delete.

Finishing It Up

The image is nearly done; a couple of quick styles will top it off nicely. Open the Layer Style dialog box for this layer (the small *fx* icon on the bottom of the Layers panel), and select Bevel And Emboss. This setting will allow for depth in the cracks. Adjust the Bevel/Emboss options as follows:

Style	Inner Bevel
Technique	Chisel Soft
Depth	1%
Direction	Down
Size	1px
Soften	0px
Use Global Light	Unchecked
Angle	120°
Altitude	10°
Gloss Contour	Default
Highlight Mode	Screen
Highlight Color	White
Highlight Opacity	28–30%
Shadow Mode	Multiply
Shadow Color	Black
Shadow Opacity	35–40%

Before closing the Layer Style dialog box, select Color Overlay from the left-hand menu. Set the color to a tan-gray, the blending mode to Color Burn, and the opacity to 15%. Click OK to accept the style.

You aren't finished with styles just yet. Select the Aged-2 layer. By manipulating an inner glow, you can add a studio-style shadow around the perimeter of the image. Open the layer styles for the Aged-2 layer and select Inner Glow. Tweak the settings for the style as follows:

Blend Mode	Multiply
Opacity	100%
Noise	0%
Color	Tan/Gray
Technique	Softer
Source	Edge
Choke	0%
Size	200%

The default settings will work for the remainder. Click OK.

If the image appears too damaged for your taste, take a soft Eraser and wipe away some of the pixels in the Cracks layer. Figure 8.12 shows the final aged photograph.

Figure 8.12 Final shot—aged and scratched

As you can see, just a few additions of paint-style qualities really enhance the final portrait. Now we will move on to generating sketches of your favorite photos. So with your mouse-pencil sharpened and ready to draw, let's continue developing that artist inside your monitor.

Photo to Line Art: Sketching

This section is a bit complicated for me as a teacher. Not that creating drawings from photographs is difficult—quite the contrary. It is an easy process, no matter which approach you take. Therein lies my problem; there are so many ways to generate line art and pencil drawings; which do I demonstrate? The variations on line-art effects could take up a book or two themselves.

For this section I've selected a method to give you a general idea of how to approach your sketches.

 Start the first technique by opening the photo of the front end of an airplane in flight. The image used here is `plane.jpg` (see Figure 8.13).

First, convert the mode of the image to Grayscale (Image → Mode → Grayscale). Duplicate the Background layer, and choose Image → Adjustments → Invert. Set the blending mode for the new layer to Color Dodge (see Figure 8.14).

Figure 8.13 How would you like to be the person who took this photo?

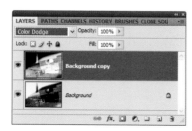

Figure 8.14 Create an inverted layer in Color Dodge blending mode

The image now appears nearly entirely white, with maybe a few spots of gray. The plane can barely be seen (if at all) as a result of creating and inverting the Color Dodge layer and interacting with the Background layer.

> The Color Dodge blending mode samples the color information in each channel and brightens the base color to reflect the blend color. This is done by decreasing the contrast.

The trick for creating a drawing is only one step away. With the Background Copy layer selected, choose Filter → Blur → Gaussian Blur. Set the radius of the blur to 5 pixels (see Figure 8.15), and take a look at the image (don't click OK just yet). The plane now appears to be drawn, with thin pencil lines outlining the contours and edges (see Figure 8.16). Different images will react differently, so you may have to adjust the amount of blur applied.

Increase the Gaussian blur to 10. The more you increase the blur, the more the layer beneath is revealed, making the lines in the drawing appear thicker and the shading more pronounced (see Figure 8.17).

Figure 8.15 *Gaussian blur for sketching*

Figure 8.16 *A light pencil sketch*

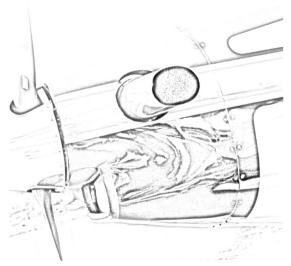

Figure 8.17 *Deeper, bolder lines*

Let's go through the process once more, only this time you will not convert the image to grayscale. Open the image young_girl.jpg (see Figure 8.18). By running through the same steps as given previously, only without the grayscale conversion, you will create a colorized line-art drawing (see Figure 8.19). The amount of blur again dictates the amount of color and sketching revealed.

Figure 8.18 *Time for a nap?*

Figure 8.19 *Pencil art colorized*

Photoshop certainly isn't limited to the use of "simple" brushes or pen tips. Any photo, shape, or object you choose can be turned into a tool with which you can paint, draw, erase, dodge, or burn. Let's move on to the next section, which describes how you can be not simply a user of tools but a creator as well.

Power of the Brush: Creating and Painting with Custom Brushes

People who are serious about their craft, hobby, or career will develop certain skill sets that allow them to succeed in that area of employment or enjoyment. They will practice, study, and learn to apply their skills in such a way that they stand out among their peers. It's a fact of life: success takes effort for most of us. There are always those fortunate few who achieve their goals with little or no effort, but they are the minority.

Something that separates a good Photoshop user from one who stands above the crowd is the ability to not only utilize the tools available in the software but recognize a need and then create her own toolsets specific to her style. Photoshop CS4 allows the designer to do exactly that: create tools that will best help her in her work aside from the canned toolbox and presets that shipped with the program.

In this section I'll demonstrate one way to utilize photos that perhaps you hadn't considered before: creating custom brushes from scratch for use in other ways. This is a teaser of sorts, as Chapter 10, "Digital Intensive: Fast and Furious Projects," discusses creating yet more presets beyond brushes. Hold on to those tired old pictures, as we use them to build your artist's toolbox.

Painting with Flowers

Open the image `rose.jpg` (Figure 8.20). A beautiful image on its own, but imagine the flower as an embellishment for other photos. Converting the photo to a brush will allow you to realize that vision in a unique way.

Before creating the brush, you should note that Photoshop CS4 will define only a brush whose largest side is 2500 pixels or less. An image with larger dimensions cannot be defined: the Define Brush Preset feature will not be available until the image is resized.

That being said, let's create a brush. This photo fits the size criteria (see Figure 8.21). A lot of the white can be trimmed away, though. You could try Edit → Trim, but I prefer extracting the flower completely from the background using the process discussed in Chapter 1, "Tools for Building Your Masterpiece." Use the Paths tool to create a path around the flower, convert the path to a selection, copy the flower, and then paste it onto a transparent background (see Figure 8.22).

Figure 8.20 Beauty in complexity

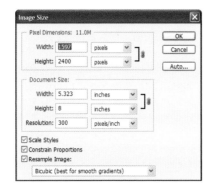

Figure 8.21 Check the size of the photo.

Figure 8.22 Extract the flower and place it on a new background.

Once the flower is on its own background at a size Photoshop will recognize as being "brushable," it is a simple matter of choosing Edit → Define Custom Brush. Name the brush as you like, and click OK (Figure 8.23). It now appears at the bottom of the Brushes panel, ready for use (Figure 8.24).

Figure 8.23 Name the new brush.

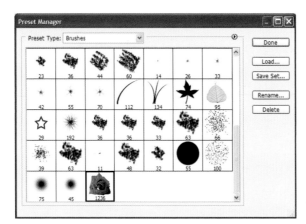

Figure 8.24 The brush now resides in the Brush tools set, ready for use.

Before painting with the brush, let's talk about saving it so you can use it later. Perhaps you would like an entire brush set consisting only of flowers. You first need to remove the other brushes, or the preloaded brushes will be included in the saved set.

To remove the unwanted brushes in one fell swoop, choose Edit → Preset Manager. In the Brushes section, select the first brush in the set. Hold down the Shift key and click on the last brush before the flower you just saved. Click Delete, and all the selected brushes will be removed, leaving only the flower. You can now save the set (recommended, as you can always add to it later). To save the set, select the Rose brush in the Preset Manager window. The Save button will be available now, as shown in Figure 8.25, and you can save the set to your computer wherever you store your Photoshop CS4 presets. It does not need to be saved to the Photoshop CS4 folder, as it can be loaded from anywhere on your computer. However, if you would like the set to appear in the menu, you will need to place it in the Brushes folder in the Photoshop/ Presets directory.

Figure 8.25 *Delete the old brushes, and save the new Flowers brush set.*

Testing the Brush

Now you are ready to give the new brush a test drive. Before working with a photo, let's try the brush on a plain black canvas. Create a new image: 12×12 inches, 300 ppi, filled with black.

Select the Brush tool, and click on the new brush. Set the foreground color to red, yellow, or something bright. Create a new layer, and click somewhere in the new layer with the brush. (See Figure 8.26.) A single click will do for this instance, but ensure the options for the brush are set to Normal, 100% Opacity and Flow.

Here's where things get interesting. Open the Brushes panel by clicking the icon on the right side of the Options bar. If you adjust a few of the brush dynamics, you can create some very interesting designs.

To start, open the Shape Dynamics dialog box. Set the Size Jitter to 80% and the Angle Jitter to 50% (see Figure 8.27). Select Scattering, check Both Axes, and set the Scatter amount to 400%.

You can apply other changes, such as Hue Jitter found under Color Dynamics, add a texture, and so on and so forth. By setting the Hue Jitter to 50% and painting on a white background a bit, I came up with the example shown in Figure 8.28. By altering the brush size to something a bit smaller and painting over a black background, you would get results similar to those in Figure 8.29.

Figure 8.26 *A single application of the new Rose brush*

Figure 8.27 *Adjust a few brush dynamics.*

Figure 8.28 Painting with the new brush

Figure 8.29 Another version on a black background

Now you can use the brush for any tool that utilizes brushes: Dodge/Burn, Eraser, and so on. You can use the brush in conjunction with masks to dress up your portraits in new and interesting way. (See Figures 8.30 and 8.31.)

Figure 8.30 Brushes and masks

Figure 8.31 Adding character to a portrait

This is just the tip of the iceberg. I hope I've given you a new way to look at brushes and that you can utilize this information as you build your own artist toolbox.

Now let's really get the artistic juices flowing. In the next section I'll demonstrate one way you can turn your personal photos into a painted portrait suitable for a gallery.

Portrait to Painting: Artistic

There are dozens of ways to achieve paint effects in Photoshop CS4, so as with sketch-style effects, deciding which paint effects to demonstrate is a tough choice. Many of the techniques forget one vital element: a realistic portrayal of what they are supposed to reflect. Realism is the focus of this project; the fine details will turn the photo into a realistic oil-on-canvas painting.

I want to take a photograph and have it appear to have been painted on a textured background sometime in the distant past. Photoshop has several tools to help you realize such a painting. The trick is to know what else is required from the toolbox to make the technique work. Sometimes all a car needs in order to turn over is a spark plug and an oil change. You have the parts and the tools; the trick is getting the pieces under the hood in the right way, saving a bundle on a mechanic.

To begin, open the image `Oldportrait.jpg` (see Figure 8.32). I've chosen this photo because of its obvious age; I think the effect will be best demonstrated as an old painting. Don't let that deter you from trying this on newer images!

Figure 8.32 *Portrait of great-great-grandpa*

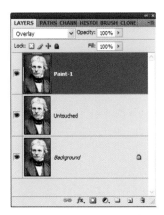

Figure 8.33 Setting up the layers/canvas

Duplicate the Background layer twice. Name the first copy **Untouched**; this will remain as named (for the time being, anyway). Name the second layer **Paint-1**; this is where you will start applying the effects. Set the blending mode for the Paint-1 layer to Overlay (see Figure 8.33).

The first layer of paint is actually an application of the Median filter to the Paint-1 layer. Choose Filter → Noise → Median, set the Radius to 8 pixels, and click OK (see Figure 8.34).

That softened the layer somewhat; now you can add some defining lines within which the paint will fall. This process is nearly a reverse of the actual painting process, but the results will be almost the same as the real thing.

Figure 8.34 The Median Noise filter acts almost like a blur.

Choose Filter → Stylize → Find Edges. Now invert the layer (⌘/Ctrl+I). See how the image (see Figure 8.35) is taking on a painted quality?

Now duplicate the Paint-1 layer; rename the new layer **Paint-2**. Set the blending mode for the layer to Soft Light, and drop the opacity to 50%. This will lighten the painting a bit, counteracting some of the darkness imposed by the Paint-1 layer.

By adjusting the Hue/Saturation for this layer, you can tweak the base paint strokes to appear as if they were laid with the same color. Trust me; it works. Choose Image → Adjustments → Hue/Saturation, enter the following settings, and click OK.

Colorize	Checked
Hue	360
Saturation	25
Lightness	0

Create another instance of the Background layer, placing it at the top of the layer stack, and name it **Paint-3**. I couldn't go through a painting exercise without using one of the paint filters, could I? Sure I could, but I'm not going to.

Set the blending mode for the new layer to Soft Light. Choose Filter → Artistic → Paint Daubs. Set both the Brush Size and Sharpness to 15, set the Brush Type to Simple, and click OK (see Figure 8.36).

Figure 8.35 Some paint-like qualities appear.

Duplicate the Untouched layer and set the opacity to 30%. Run the Paint Daubs filter once more on this layer. Rename the layer **Base Paint** (see Figure 8.37).

That's a pretty fair painting, but thus far the canvas being painted on has no texture. As I said, this is actually being painted nearly in reverse. The pixels needed to be in place prior to manipulating them into a canvas.

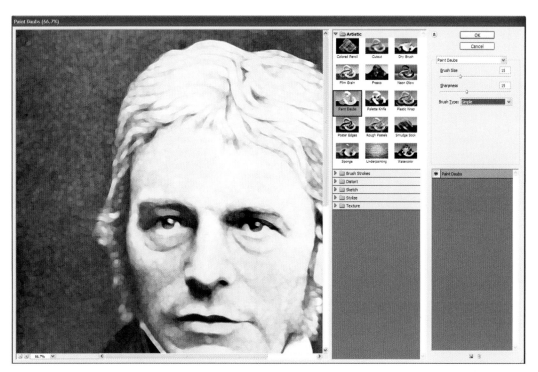

Figure 8.36 *Paint Daubs dialog box*

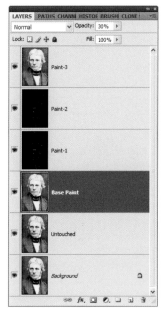

Figure 8.37 *Rename the working layer to Base Paint.*

Figure 8.38 *Select a portion of the face in the Color Range dialog box.*

Select the Untouched layer. I just can't leave it untouched; something has to be done. This layer will provide the foundation for the canvas. Choose Select → Color Range. Select an area in the face (see Figure 8.38). Quite a bit will come up in the selection, but no worries. It needs to be that way (see Figure 8.39).

With the selection active, open the Channels panel and select the RGB channel. Run the Paint Daubs filter again, this time setting the Brush Size to 5 and the Sharpness to 10. Stay with the Simple Brush and click OK.

Choose Filter → Texture → Texturizer. Select Canvas for the texture, and set the Scaling to 100% and the Relief to 5. Click OK.

Run the Texturizer one more time with the same settings as before. The image now appears to have a rough surface similar to those used in standard oil paintings (see Figures 8.40 and 8.41).

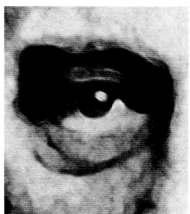

Figure 8.40 *A rough canvas surface is applied to the new painting.*

Figure 8.39 *The active selection*

Figure 8.41 *The new canvas in full view*

It almost looks good enough to frame, don't you think? Try this process on your family portraits... perfect to send as holiday gifts to relatives!

Summary

There are a few third-party software packages out there that claim to do much of what this chapter has covered. I'm of the mind that Photoshop CS4 gives you plenty of tools to achieve artistic renderings all on its own, so saving the extra expense and learning how to do this with the tools at hand is easier on the budget. As a bonus, you learn more about the software along the way.

Now let's take all this knowledge and go a bit wacky. In the next chapter we'll create some very cool portraits, manipulating the subjects well beyond what nature intended.

nine

People as Art: Digital Manipulation

I make no pretense of being *an artist of any vein outside of computers, other than where my photography is concerned. Photoshop is a tool that releases the inner artist in those who, like me, have brains that are creative to a fault but lose it when attempting to re-create the visions with a pencil or paintbrush. Photoshop has given digital artists new media in which to work, media that real-world artists would never have considered possible years ago. Some artists use the human body as a canvas; digital artists can use it as their clay. We can shape it, mold it, color it, add appendages or remove them, with no harm to the model. (If the model sees the art, some harm may come to the artist, but I digress.)*

    This chapter is specifically about using the human form as a medium for artistic molding and manipulation. You will color it, texture it, melt it, and mold it. Of all the chapters in this book, this is the one closest to my heart because the manipulations in this chapter are from my imagination, working with the medium I love. In this chapter you get to open my head and see the right side of my brain, and in the process I hope you will pick up some ideas of how to apply what you see to your own work. Grab your magnifying glass, screw off the top of my skull, brush away the cobwebs, and see what makes me tick.

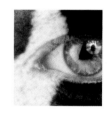

    The images referenced as source files for these techniques can be found in the Chapter 9 Source Files *folder on this book's CD.*

Checkered Woman

I categorize this piece as impressionistic, but the art being formed varies from the original definition. Impressionism took shape in France in the 1870s. The focus was the initial visual impression of a work, with the primary elements of the style being unmixed primary colors and small strokes that simulated reflected light.

This piece may better be categorized as digital impressionism. Stark primary colors come into play, and lighting is of the essence; the medium is photography and how these elements work together in a photo intended to generate instant reactions.

What I see in my mind's eye is a woman whose body paint mimics the pattern on the wall behind her. I think of those people who endure hours of having their bodies painted for Mardi Gras. Like the whole tattoo issue, I just gotta ask, "Why in the world...?" At the same time, the body-paint idea offers inspiration for this technique, but you get the effect without having to spend hours having your body painted.

To realize this effect, only two images are needed: the subject and the background that the subject will attempt to blend with. Photoshop and you will do the rest.

Open the images `wallpose.jpg` and `checkers.jpg` (see Figures 9.1 and 9.2).

Figure 9.1 Bahamas vacation

Figure 9.2 Checkers, anyone?

Following the well-practiced extraction techniques, extract the model from her background. You may either copy her and paste her into the checkerboard image or place the checkerboard image in her document. Either way, ensure that she appears above the background, as shown in Figure 9.3.

Duplicate the checkered layer and move it to the top of the layer stack. Name this layer **CheckerOverlay**, as shown in Figure 9.4.

Click on the CheckerOverlay layer and change the blending mode to Hue (see Figure 9.5). This will cause the color to disappear, leaving it black-and-white. I would like to retain some color, and once again Blend If is going to help. Open the layer styles for the CheckerOverlay layer and, with Blend If: Gray selected, move the Black slider for This Layer to 10 (see Figure 9.6). Click OK.

Something else you can try during this process is to create a displacement map of the woman as done in earlier chapters and apply it to the checker pattern. I've done this for the example image to show what it could look like.

Figure 9.4 Duplicate the checkered layer.

Figure 9.5 Blending-mode change

Figure 9.3 Extract the model and replace the background.

Figure 9.6 Our old friend, Blend If

This adjustment wipes away the color where the white checkers overlay the skin, but the color is retained where the black overlays the skin, as shown in Figure 9.7.

From this point you have a fair foundational image to alter and tweak as you like, and simple blending mode and Opacity changes will yield some interesting results. For instance, open the Styles dialog box for the CheckerOverlay layer and select the Blending Options. Change the blending mode from Hue to Difference. You will get an alternating Mod-Art effect, as shown in Figure 9.8.

Figure 9.7 *The white overlay removes color; black retains it.*

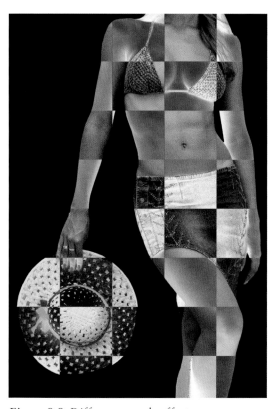

Figure 9.8 *Difference-mode effect*

Move the White Underlying Layer slider to the left slightly, and the white squares reappear, with those areas of the model inverted from her original color (see Figure 9.9).

Want to show only the altered Difference portions of the model? Select the model layer and change the blending mode to Multiply (Figure 9.10). Or you may choose to show the other portions of her body, which you may do by changing the model's blending mode to Lighten (Figure 9.11).

I use this exercise in the real world to help people wrap their minds around blending modes and the variant effects they can give us. Not an example many photographers will use in the real world, I'll grant you. But some do use very similar effects in advertising work, and this helps whet the whistle, so to speak.

Let's take this concept of radical retouching a step further. Next up is a curious little experiment in applying animal patterns to the human body.

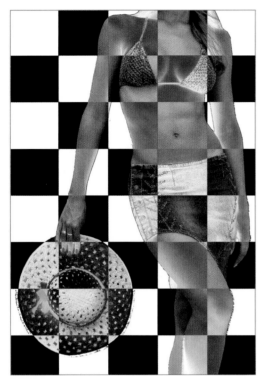

Figure 9.9 *Return of the white checkers*

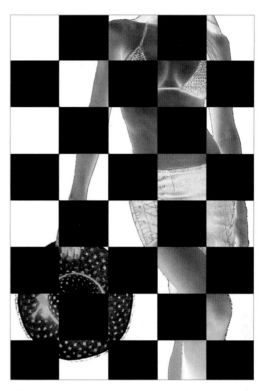

Figure 9.10 *Variation 1*

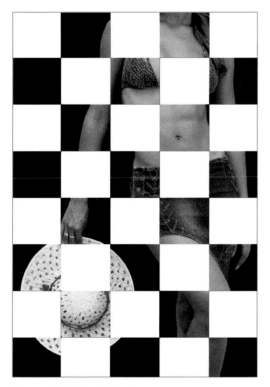

Figure 9.11 *Variation 2*

Zebra-Woman

This technique is similar to the previous one. This time, however, the texture being applied is a pattern out of nature rather than geometric textiles.

The concept is this: merge a pattern taken from nature with a human face. The convergence of two elements from the natural world will help to put forth the feeling of intelligence combined with a wild element. Unlike the last piece, this project I see as a facial close-up. The primary subject will have a smart yet feral appearance. I also see a lot of color in natural tones to help the end effect. Following the same idea (if not the same process) as the Checkered Woman exercise, this will be a piece of cake to realize. One hopes, anyway!

To begin, open the images `really.jpg` and `zebra.jpg` (see Figures 9.12 and 9.13). Copy the zebra and paste it into a new layer over the woman. Resize the zebra layer with the Transform tools so that the fur pattern covers the woman's skin, as shown in Figure 9.14. I've reduced the opacity of the Zebra layer as a guide to see that the entire face is covered. Feel free to do the same; then increase the opacity once the transformation has been completed.

Figure 9.13 *Borrowing a pattern from nature*

Figure 9.12 *You are going to turn me into* what?

Figure 9.14 *Conform the zebra pattern to the face image by using the Transform tools.*

The following steps will come fast and furious, as you should be an old hand at them by now. Duplicate the Background layer. Shut off the Zebra layer. Create a displacement map of the woman's face and save it to your hard disk (see Figures 9.15 and 9.16). Turn the Zebra layer on again, and displace it by using the newly created displacement map (see Figure 9.17).

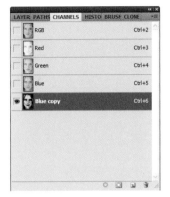

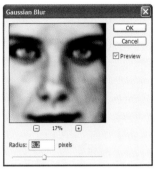

Figure 9.15 Creating a channel for the displacement map

Figure 9.16 Blurring the channel

Figure 9.17 Displacing the fur

In order for the skin of the woman's face to appear as though the zebra pattern belongs there naturally, you need to remove or alter the color beneath the stripes in some way. A Hue/Saturation layer with a mask that displays only the black stripes (in other words, the black stripes in the pattern are visible, or colored white, in the mask) with the Saturation slider moved all the way to the left, remove color from that area of the woman's face in the layer below. Create the Hue/Saturation adjustment layer between the Background Copy layer and the zebra-pattern layer, or Layer 1. See Figure 9.18.

In the next step, create a mask for the zebra-pattern layer, or Layer 1 in this case. With a feathered brush, paint with black in the mask over the areas where the woman's hair is shown. This will reveal her natural hair from the Background Copy layer, while leaving the zebra pattern on her face. Next, select a smaller brush without much feather to the edges and paint over the eyes and lips in the mask. Again, this will reveal the natural eyes and lips.

Change the blending mode for the zebra-pattern layer to Soft Light. Duplicate this layer twice, and apply a slight Gaussian blur to one of the pattern layers. You may also increase the contrast between the whites and blacks by creating a Levels adjustment layer and manipulating the sliders for greater contrast. You will want to ensure that only the white areas of the pattern are manipulated by the Levels adjustment. In the Levels adjustment layer's mask, paint over the hair, eyes, lips, and black stripes with black. Then make your Levels adjustment. When all these steps are completed, the Layers palette should look something like Figure 9.19.

Figure 9.18 A Hue/Saturation layer is used to remove the woman's face color beneath the black stripes.

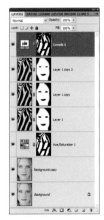

Figure 9.19 The Zebra-Woman thus far

You have just a short way to go. Click on the Background Copy layer, and set the blending mode to Overlay (see Figure 9.20). This will help bring out the color in the overall piece. Next, create a new layer at the top of the layer stack, and set the blending mode to Color. Set the foreground color to a nice earth tone, and paint over the irises with a small brush, taking away the blue and replacing it with a wilder, more feral hue (see Figure 9.21). Figure 9.22 shows my final image.

Work with the masks to better define areas in the image you think need touching up. You may also opt to reduce the opacity of any of the normal or adjustment layers, darken the borders, and so on and so forth. I'll trust your judgment from here on.

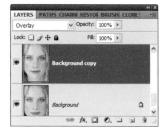

Figure 9.20 *A blending change deepens the color of the overall image.*

Figure 9.21 *Giving her eyes a wilder tone*

To realize this final image, you didn't really use any new tricks beyond what you've seen in the rest of the book. This is key: more often than not the techniques to achieve different effects are the same—only the way they are applied changes. Again, this is where imagination and learning curve meet.

Now let's really exercise our inner Frankenstein. In the next section we'll take a mild-mannered model and turn him into a more advanced version of himself.

Figure 9.22
Zebra-woman realized

Cyborg: Digital Distortions

A few years ago, I coauthored a book with my good friend Colin Smith called *Photoshop Most Wanted*, in which I demonstrated one way to turn a person into a cyborg. In that tutorial, I used the Borg from the *Star Trek* franchise as the foundation for the technique.

In this section I want to revisit the cyborg, but this time with an entirely different approach. In the aforementioned book, I was looking for photorealism in my cyborg. With this approach, I want to stay close to the types of effects you've already seen in this title. There are a couple of cool things I'm going to show you in this technique that I have not approached elsewhere. I hope you enjoy this trek into my imagination.

Preparing the Head

Begin by opening the image `contemplate.jpg` (see Figure 9.23). As you can already tell, I am a fan of head shots; the personality and structure of the face and head of my subjects lend themselves to the creative process and often serve as inspiration for the final piece. In this instance, I took one look at this man's head and thought, "Wouldn't it be cool if the top of his skull were made of metal?" Granted, this is probably not something that would pop into everybody's head, probably not even into a fraction of people's heads. Some days it's fun to be me.

Once again you start by duplicating the Background layer (see Figure 9.24). I want to pull off the top of this man's head, so the first part of this process is to create a thin dark line around the man's head (see Figure 9.25). The Burn tool with a 16-pixel round, slightly feathered brush with the range set to Midtones and Exposure to 50% will work perfectly in this instance. Draw a line around the man's head by using the Burn tool. You may need to make a couple passes over the line with the brush to darken it a bit.

Figure 9.24 Duplicate the Background layer.

Figure 9.23 A contemplative stare

Figure 9.25 Burn a curved line around the man's skull.

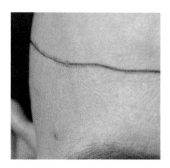

Figure 9.26 The Pucker tool in the Liquify dialog box is used to create a seam or scar.

Right now the Burn line probably just looks like someone took an eyeliner pencil and drew a ring around the skull. The Pucker tool in the Liquify filter dialog box will help pinch the line together, making it appear more like a scar or seam rather than a drawn line. With a narrow brush, use the Liquify filter to tighten the line around the man's head. Where the line meets the background, use the Pucker tool to draw in the side, making it appear as though the side of his head were dented. This helps add to the illusion. See Figure 9.26.

I've not touched on much photorealism in this book, in particular making metal out of nothing, as I have done in other books. I can't let this slip by; metals are some of my favorite effects. Let's create rivets to bolt the two pieces of the man's skull together.

When you attempt to generate metal effects, curves are really going to make those metallic characteristics stand out. When adjusting curves on a gradual grayscale gradient, you can really bring out the metal, especially if your curve has a wave to it (brighten the darks, darken the midtones, and so on.)

Create a new layer and rename it **Rivets** (see Figure 9.27). Using the Elliptical Marquee tool, draw oval/round selections, and fill them with a gray-to-dark-gray radial gradient. On the side of the head, the rivets will be oval because you are looking at them from an angled perspective (see Figure 9.28). As you create rivets on the front of the forehead, they will be round. For a tighter rivet effect, adjust the curves for the Rivet layer. Use Figure 9.29 as a guide for the Curves adjustment, and click OK. This will give you a greater separation between the light and the black, making the radial gradients appear more like rivets. See Figure 9.30.

Figure 9.27 Rivets layer

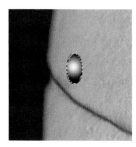

Figure 9.28 A radial gradient serves as the foundation for the rivets.

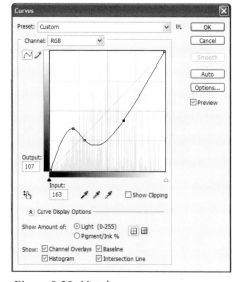

Figure 9.29 Metal curve

Figure 9.30 Skullcap fastened firmly in place

To turn the top portion of the skull into metal, that portion needs to be separated from the rest of the man's head. Using the Polygonal Lasso tool with zero feather, select the top portion of the man's head along the seam and separate it from the background. Choose Layer → New → Layer Via Cut. Name the new layer **SkullCap**. It should be located beneath the Rivets layer in the Layers panel (see Figure 9.31).

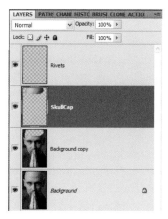

The color needs to be removed from the SkullCap layer in order for the metal effect to work. Adjust the Hue/Saturation of the SkullCap layer, decreasing the Saturation to –100. Click OK. Adjust the curves for this layer as well, using Figure 9.32 as a guide, and click OK. You may want to use the Burn tool to darken the edges of the plate on the shadowed side of the face. The result should be close to that shown in Figure 9.33. The top of the man's head should appear as though a metal plate is bolted or riveted to it.

Figure 9.31 *Separate the skullcap from the head.*

If anyone ever tells you that human flesh cannot be turned into metal, now you have proof to the contrary. Photoshop makes a lot of things possible that were previously unheard of.

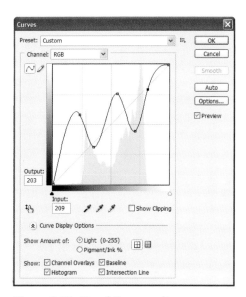

Figure 9.32 *Metal Curves adjustment*

Figure 9.33 *Skin and bone are replaced by stainless steel.*

Relocating the Subject

The creation of the scar, the removal of the top of the head, and the conversion of the skin to metal were the primary techniques I wanted to demonstrate in this exercise. The following steps have been demonstrated a couple of times (in some cases many times) throughout the book, so I won't spend additional space explaining what's going on; you have seen and performed this technique before. I do, however, want to dress up this image a bit and complete the cyborg, so please try to follow along visually.

The next action you're going to perform is to extract the man from his background and create a new background by using a green-to-black radial gradient (see Figure 9.34). With a Hue/Saturation adjustment layer at the top of the layer stack, remove some of the saturation from the man's face and body, and tweak the color a bit for a slightly less natural tone, perhaps +9 for Hue and −55 for Saturation.

Figure 9.34 Separate the man from the background, and replace the red with a green-to-black radial gradient.

You are now going to borrow another image and use it to dress up portions of the cyborg image. Open techrings.jpg (see Figure 9.35). Copy the entire image and paste it below the extracted man layer. Set the blending mode to Overlay.

Duplicate this layer, and drag that copy above the extracted man layer. With the Transform tools, reduce the size of this layer and position it so that it resides over the man's right eye (see Figure 9.36). Trim away the edges so that only the eye is covered. The Eraser tool will work in this instance, or the Marquee tools, a mask, and so on—it's your call. Set the blending mode for this layer to Linear Light. See Figure 9.37.

Figure 9.35 Tech elements borrowed from another image

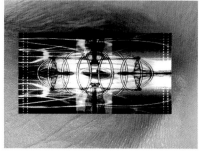

Figure 9.36 Adding digital effects to the eye

Figure 9.37 Blending change to Linear Light

The image `circuit.jpg` will also assist in digitizing this person. Open it now (see Figure 9.38). Copy and paste it into a new layer in the man image at the top of the layer stack. ⌘/Ctrl-click the extracted man layer and select Inverse. Delete the circuits from the background, leaving them to cover only the man. Expose the left eye by creating a mask and painting over the eye in the mask with black. Change the blending mode for the Circuits layer to Overlay (see Figure 9.39).

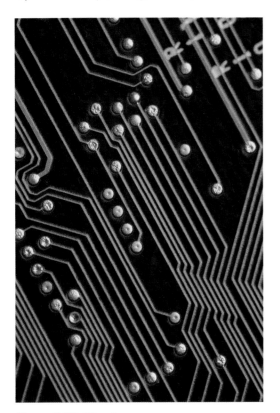

Figure 9.38 Circuits

Figure 9.39 Circuits cover the man, not the eye or the background.

A quick Levels adjustment will help you adjust the contrast. Move the center slider to the right and the White, or right-hand, slider to the left, stopping where that color information begins to climb in the Levels dialog box (Figure 9.40). Selecting the man's shirt and hands with the Marquee tools, you can further increase contrast and make those parts darker by using Levels (see Figure 9.41).

To finalize this example, simply go back through the layers with Dodge/Burn and paint in the masks to generate your final composite. You may want to add a layer in Color mode to generate some green reflections on the metal. My final image is shown in Figure 9.42.

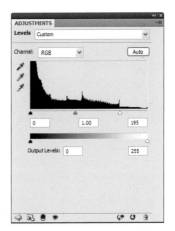

Figure 9.40 Levels adjustment

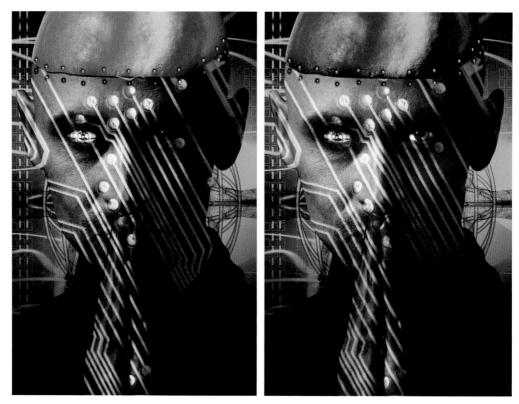

Figure 9.41 Darkening the shirt and hands   *Figure 9.42 Final image*

This was a fairly radical experiment but a good exercise for tying previously learned techniques into one composite. Next we'll delve into the realm of photorealistic blending, merging two distinct texture types into a combined melding effect. So without further ado, let's create a statue.

Flesh to Stone

As my mind visualizes this piece, I see a gradual transition of flesh to marble. Recalling a bit of mythology as well as a few old movies, a vision of a Medusa turning her victims to stone with her gaze comes to mind. What if that Medusa had fallen in love with her victim? Realizing too late that his fate had been sealed by her adoring stare, she opts to share his fate, embracing his statuesque form and then casting her spell upon herself. Okay, this may seem like a scene from a bad romance novel, but it will serve well for this particular project.

First, open the image hug.jpg (see Figure 9.43). This photo lends itself well to the effect I envision, because skin dominates the majority of the photo. Something that just came to mind is that the end result would be more effective if a portion of the "statue" were removed as though broken. A finger should work nicely.

Duplicate the Background layer and rename it **Couple**. Duplicate the Couple layer. Use the Clone Stamp to wipe away a portion of the index finger and the shadow from the finger with skin from the man's back. Use the Burn tool to darken the edge of the finger, as shown in Figure 9.44.

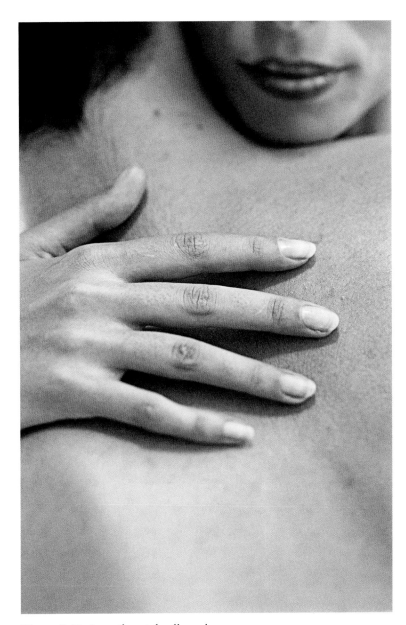

Figure 9.43 *A gentle yet deadly embrace*

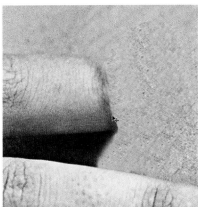

Figure 9.44 *Break off the index finger.*

Use the Marquee tools to create a selection at the end of the finger extending just beyond the broken edge. Make a Brightness/Contrast adjustment to that area, darkening the selected portion significantly. (See Figures 9.45 and 9.46.)

Now open the image `veined_marble.jpg` (see Figure 9.47). Because you will be using Apply Image to apply this image to the couple, both images need to be the same dimensions. Resize the marble image to match the exact dimensions of the couple, as shown in Figure 9.48.

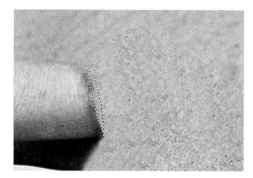

Figure 9.45 Make a selection at the break-off point.

Figure 9.46 Darken the selected area.

Figure 9.47 Marble photo

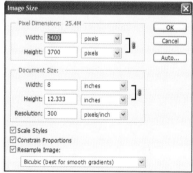

Figure 9.48 Resize the marble photo.

Select the Couple copy layer (see Figure 9.49) and choose Image → Apply Image (see Figure 9.50). Note that you will need to select veined_marble.jpg as the source image. Set the rest of the Apply Image attributes as shown in the figure.

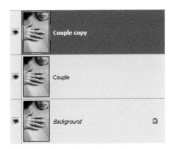

Figure 9.49 *Get ready for the metamorphosis.*

Figure 9.50 *Apply Image settings*

Figure 9.51 shows the result of applying the marble texture to the couple. I find this interesting because the veins in the stone maintain the same pattern on both individuals.

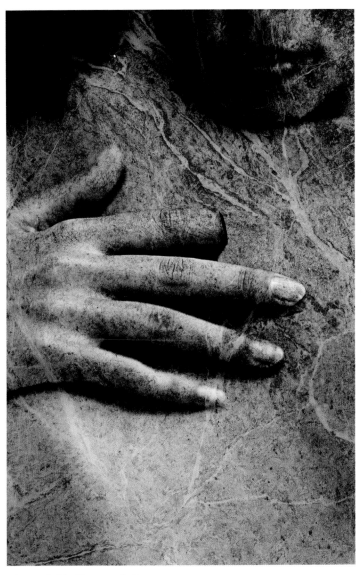

Figure 9.51 *The couple in stone*

Now create a mask for the Couple copy layer. There should be a point in the image where the flesh appears to be gradually changing to stone to remain true to the original concept. A mask will work great here, because another unedited version of the couple already resides beneath the one merged with stone. With the mask selected, set the foreground color to black, and paint over the back of the woman's hand, extending up the fingers a short way but not to the point where the finger is broken. The result should look like Figure 9.52.

Just a couple of finishing touches, and you are all set. First, choose Image → Adjustments → Hue/Saturation, and decrease the Saturation of the Couple layer to −90. You may also adjust the color of the rock at this point with the Hue adjustment slider, but try to reach a nice granite hue, perhaps +6 for Hue and +2 for Lightness.

Next, you can burn a few cracks into the stone with the Burn tool set to Shadows (with a Brush Size of 19 and Exposure set to 50%) and applied to darker portions or veins in the marble (see Figure 9.53).

Figure 9.52 Transition from flesh to rock

Figure 9.53 *A sweet yet sorrowful goodbye*

Summary

I hope you've enjoyed this chapter on extreme digital manipulation. If nothing else was accomplished, this chapter did demonstrate a classic right-brained approach to Photoshop. If you can imagine it, chances are you can also build it, and do it in such a way as to trick the mind into seeing what shouldn't be possible in the real world. We aren't looking for truth, however. We are looking to tap an artistic vein.

Chapter 10 will go further in the process, challenging you to think about a straight-forward program in a few very unconventional ways. We'll look at more photorealism and even teach you to convert your images into tools to be used in creating other images. Chapter 10 is, almost literally, a crash course in creativity.

ten

Digital Intensive:
Fast and Furious Projects

You've covered a lot of material *in the first*
nine chapters, learning quite a bit of information regarding techniques,
processes, and their application in Photoshop to create desired results. Up
to this point I've approached each technique with a specific result in mind,
demonstrating the techniques, filters, and so forth I would use to achieve
that final effect.

This chapter is certainly similar in that regard. What I intend in this
chapter that is a bit different is to have the end project in mind rather than
the process, going from point A to point Z and achieving something that
can be used to fill the portfolio and not just the designer's toolbox. In
reality the previous chapters were exercises to get your hands dirty in the
program so you could become more confident, begin thinking outside the
box, jump the hurdles on the learning curve, and begin thinking about
Photoshop intuitively rather than with trepidation. Once you get to that
point, projects like these become much easier to tackle.

The layout of these techniques is in numbered steps, or standard
"cookbook" format. Though there may be a lot of steps in the techniques
shown here, I'm slimming down the commentary and diving right into the
process of each. So if you are ready to begin, have Photoshop open, have a
hot cup o' coffee (or whatever beverage you choose) close at hand, and
let's get started.

The images referenced as source files for these techniques can be
found in the Chapter 10 Source Files *folder on this book's CD.*

Project 1: Photorealistic Framing

It's a relatively simple matter to print your images, purchase a suitable frame, and showcase them physically in your home, a gallery, or wherever. What about framing images for display online or via a digital medium such as a slideshow on CD/DVD, a PowerPoint presentation, or some other electronic venue? Scanning photo frames can be a bit of a pain, without a doubt.

For the first project in this chapter I'll demonstrate the creation of a photorealistic frame, or rather a frame that looks like it could exist in the real world. Photoshop isn't simply a program to correct or manipulate "real" pictures; you can also create the embellishments for those photos, as you will see in this and the second project in this chapter.

Figures 10.1 and 10.2 are examples of the frame style we'll tackle. Granted, your end result may not be exactly like these examples, but variation is okay in this regard.

Figure 10.1 My wonderful kids in full frame

Figure 10.2 A close-up of the frame style

One more thing before I get started. As with most things done in Photoshop, this process can be recorded as an action as well, with the usual nonactionable limitations (painting and the like). As you begin building your frames, if you are familiar with action creation you may want to record the process so you can create the frame for other photos at a later date by simply running the action instead of building it again from scratch. My website (www.actionfx.com) has many video tutorials regarding action creation, so you may want to check it out.

To start, open the image Ali_Noah-2008.tif on the book's CD.

Preparing the Image

1. Double-click the Background layer to convert it to a normal layer. The new layer will be named Layer 0 by default.
2. Choose Image → Canvas Size. Increase the Width and Height by 50 pixels each, with the Relative checkbox checked. Click OK (see Figure 10.3). Your image will now have a transparent border around the edge.
3. Create a new layer and move it beneath Layer 0. Fill this layer (Edit → Fill) with 50% gray at 100% opacity. Click OK.
4. Create another layer, move it to the bottom of the layer stack, increase the canvas size by 100 pixels in both Width and Height, and fill the new layer with 50% gray.
5. Repeat the process in step 4 once more, only this time increase the canvas size by 50 pixels in Width and Height. When finished, you will have three gray-filled layers beneath the photo layer, as shown in Figure 10.4.

Building the Frame Texture

6. Create a new layer and place it at the bottom of the layer stack. Do not fill this layer with anything just yet.
7. Change the foreground color to the following:

Red   130
Green   100
Blue   64

Likewise, change the background color to the following:

Red   106
Green   63
Blue   31

Both are earth tones, which will aid in the frame's creation.

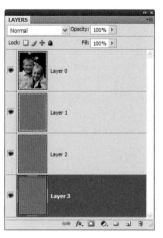

Figure 10.3 *Increase the size of the canvas.*

Figure 10.4 *The Layers arrangement thus far*

8. Select Filter → Render → Clouds. This fills the bottom layer with a cloud pattern using the foreground and background colors. It isn't visible just yet, but we will change that in short order. If you would like to see what is happening in the next few steps, feel free to turn off the gray layers and the photo for the time being.

9. Duplicate the clouds layer. Choose Filter → Render → Difference Clouds. Run this filter six times on the layer. This helps create a greater distinction between the browns, which will help in texturing and coloring the frame. (See Figure 10.5.)

10. Merge the bottom two layers (Layer → Merge Down).

11. Run the Dry Brush filter twice on this layer (Filter → Artistic → Dry Brush) with the following settings:

Brush Size   10
Texture   0
Detail   3

12. Choose Filter → Sharpen → Unsharp Mask. Enter the following settings, and click OK:

Amount   350%
Radius   1.2px
Threshold   0

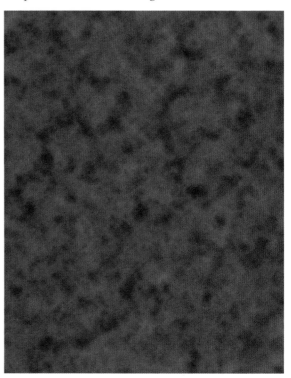

Figure 10.5 *The pattern thus far*

The emerging pattern consists of distinct separations between the colors, giving a strata effect or one you might see in topography maps. This will play well as the texture for the frame that's taking shape (Figure 10.6).

With the pattern generated to give the frame its overall feel, we can now move on to building the frame itself.

Layering the Frame Elements

Remember those multiple gray layers we created a couple pages ago? The texture we generated now needs to be duplicated a couple times in the size of those gray layers:

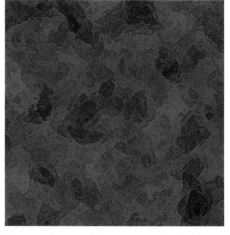

Figure 10.6 *Building texture for the frame*

1. Stay on the texture layer, but ⌘/Ctrl-click on Layer 2.

2. Copy the selection and paste it into a new layer.

3. Repeat the process with gray Layer 1, pasting the smaller selection into a layer above the last.

Don't worry about the gray layers; just leave them turned off. (See Figure 10.7.)

So which Photoshop feature can give us distinct beveled edges? You guessed it. Layer Styles will take the frame where it needs to go. We'll start with the bottom layer. Highlight the bottom texture layer and click the *fx* button on the bottom of the Layers panel to open the style settings for that layer. Beginning with Bevel And Emboss, enter the following settings (see Figure 10.8.):

Style	Inner Bevel
Technique	Chisel Hard
Depth	530%
Direction	Up
Size	20px
Soften	0px
Angle	–135°
Use Global Light	Checked
Altitude	30°
Gloss Contour	Linear (default)
Anti-aliased	Unchecked
Highlight Mode	Screen
Highlight Color	White
Highlight Opacity	75%
Shadow Mode	Multiply
Shadow Color	Black
Shadow Opacity	75%

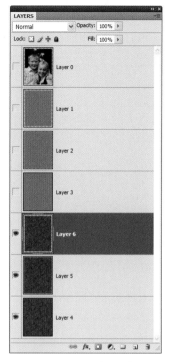

Figure 10.7 *Stacking the frame layers*

Now move on to the Contour settings. This adjustment is what really pushes the frame's beveled edge into the real world, as opposed to simply looking like a canned Photoshop bevel setting. Select Contour from the left side of the Styles dialog box, and click directly over the small contour window to bring up the Contour Editor. Using the mouse, create a contour similar to that shown in Figure 10.9. Keep an eye on the edge of your image while you work to see the effect as you adjust this setting. When you are happy with the edge, move on to the

Gradient Overlay. Create an alternating light-to-dark metal-style gradient, or simply apply the default copper gradient with an angle of 30, 120, or something that places the gradient on the image at an off-center angle. Set the blending mode for the gradient to Overlay, or if that is too dark, set it to Soft Light. I'll leave this to your taste, but in my example I've set it to Overlay with a reduced opacity of 60%. Accept the changes to the styles by clicking OK.

Figure 10.8 *Beveling the frame's outer edge*

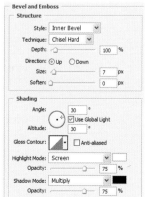

Figure 10.9 *Contours build character.*

Bypass Layer 5 and move up to Layer 6. Open the Style dialog box for this layer, and select the Bevel And Emboss settings. Enter the following:

Style	Inner Bevel
Technique	Chisel Hard
Depth	100%
Direction	Up
Size	7px
Soften	0px
Angle	30°
Use Global Light	Checked
Altitude	30°
Gloss Contour	Linear (default)
Anti-aliased	Unchecked
Highlight Mode	Screen
Highlight Color	White
Highlight Opacity	75%
Shadow Mode	Multiply
Shadow Color	Black
Shadow Opacity	75%

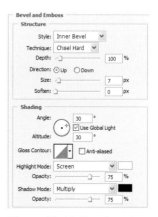

Figure 10.10 Bevel settings

Figure 10.10 shows the Bevel And Emboss settings as they should appear in the Styles dialog box. As before, move on to the Contour settings. Create another contour, similar to that shown in Figure 10.11. This is just a slight variant from the one you created for the previous layer.

1. Select Inner Glow first, and enter the following settings (Figure 10.12).:

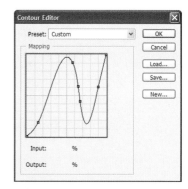

Figure 10.11 Another contour

Blend Mode	Multiply
Opacity	85%
Noise	0%
Color	Black
Technique	Softer
Source	Edge
Choke	0%
Size	75px

2. Select Gradient Overlay on the left side of the Styles dialog box, and load or create a metal-style gradient of alternating light grays and dark grays, as shown in Figure 10.13.
3. Set the blending mode to Overlay, the style to Linear, the angle to 118–120 degrees, and the scale to 100%. Click OK.

Figure 10.14 shows the frame thus far.

Figure 10.12 Using Inner Glow for shading

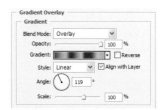

Figure 10.13 Using Gradient Overlay to add highlights

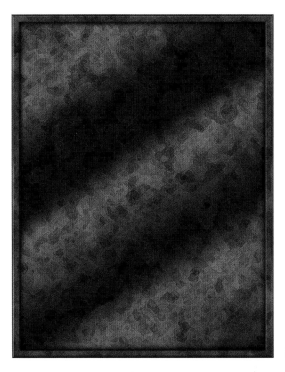

Figure 10.14 *The frame thus far*

Let's create one more layer before we get down to the matting:

1. Duplicate the last layer we worked on (Layer 6).
2. ⌘/Ctrl-click the new layer to generate a selection around it.
3. Choose Select → Modify → Contract, and enter a setting of **100**.
4. Choose Select → Inverse and press Delete.

Since the layer already had a style applied to it, the bevel will be in place.

Turn on the photo layer. We'll need to make it fit inside the innermost beveled layer, with some space around it to add the mat:

1. Select the photo layer, and choose Edit → Transform → Scale.
2. On the Options bar change both the Width and the Height settings to 90%. Accept the transformation.
3. Now open the Styles dialog box for the photo layer. Go to the Stroke settings and enter the following (see Figure 10.15):

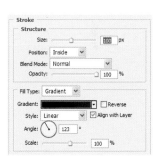

Figure 10.15 *Using a Stroke gradient to add a mat*

Size	100px
Position	Inside
Blend Mode	Normal
Opacity	100%
Fill Type	Gradient
Gradient Colors	Use a standard gradient, but use black as the first color (0 position Color Stop) and an almost-black shade of gray for the 100% color stop.
Angle	120–125%
Scale	100%

This gives the illusion of matting to border the photo (see Figure 10.16).

Figure 10.16 *Choosing the gradient colors*

The mat portion needs to be inset, which we can do quickly by applying a Bevel And Emboss adjustment:

1. Select Bevel And Emboss, and enter the following (as shown in Figure 10.17):

Style	Inner Bevel
Technique	Smooth
Depth	100%
Direction	Down
Size	2px
Soften	0px
Angle	30°
Use Global Light	Checked
Altitude	30°
Gloss Contour	Linear (default)
Anti-aliased	Unchecked
Highlight Mode	Screen
Highlight Color	White
Highlight Opacity	75%
Shadow Mode	Multiply
Shadow Color	Black
Shadow Opacity	75%

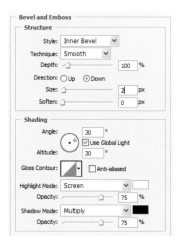

Figure 10.17 Beveling to inset the mat

2. Click OK to apply the style to the layer.

Figure 10.18 shows the result of this adjustment.

Some variation in light, shadow, or saturation between the frame's layers will add to the end effect. Think about seeing such an object in the real world, hanging on a wall or sitting on a piano. The color aspect changes as you move about a room. The position of an overhead light or corner lamp will alter your impression of the object, as will distance, time of day, and a host of other variables. To increase the realism in the frame, we simply introduce one or two of those variables into the mix to help distinguish our object from other digital creations.

For this example we'll add a Gradient adjustment:

1. Select Layer 6 copy (or the layer directly below the topmost frame layer).

2. Open the Adjustments dialog box via the icon on the bottom of the Layers panel, and select Gradient Map (Figure 10.19).

3. Use a standard back-to-white default gradient (Figure 10.20), and change the blending mode to Overlay.

4. Reduce the opacity of the Gradient Map layer to 40–60%, depending on your personal taste.

Figure 10.18 The result on the image

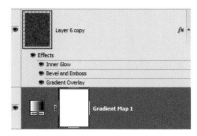

Figure 10.19 Add variety between the frame layers using a gradient.

One more small touchup that will assist in creating realistic qualities for the framed photo is to add slight glass reflections to the face of the photo. Create a layer at the top of the layer stack, and set the blending mode to Screen. Using either a gradient (white-to-transparent) or simply painting with white using a soft, round brush, paint over the corners of the photo, avoiding the frame. You can isolate your painting by ⌘/Ctrl-clicking the photo layer to generate a selection around that area before painting (see Figure 10.21).

When all is said and done, you should have a framed photo suitable for hanging on a real wall (if it were real, that is). Figure 10.22 shows my final image. Yours should be relatively close to the example shown.

Something else you can try as you make your own version is adding or subtracting frame layers, creating metal effects on one of the layers, adding a wood texture, and tweaking the bevel settings for increasing or decreasing depth. There are really no limits to what you can achieve—just go into the project with the thought of how light and color play in a real-world setting, and go from there.

Now we'll move on to a favorite subject of mine, and we'll stretch the boundaries of creativity a bit by using a photo to create actual tools to use in other Photoshop projects.

Figure 10.21 *Add white reflections in a new layer.*

Figure 10.20 *The default black-to-white gradient will work perfectly in this instance.*

Figure 10.22 *A framed photo Grandma would be proud to display*

Project 2: Changing Photos into Photoshop Presets

Photoshop presets have been very good to me, as they started my trek into the world of digital manipulation, which turned into a career that has sustained my family for better than 10 years. Along the way I've delved further into photography, into writing, and into creating training videos and such, and fortunately all of these things meld together into a very satisfying career.

Photoshop CS4 comes with many presets, or custom tools and settings, that you can use in your work. What I've found over the years is the tools made by others, while in many cases very helpful, are not always the perfect tools for the job. When you find yourself in this situation, it is good to stretch your imagination a bit and exercise Photoshop's ability to create custom tools. In fact, a single image can be turned into a variety of tools, allowing you to rapidly fill your toolbox.

To demonstrate, I scanned a leaf I picked this morning from the maple tree in my backyard, and I've provided this file for your use: `Leaf.tif` on the book's CD. Knowing that the higher the resolution, the better the preset (especially in the case of custom shapes), I scanned the image at 300 dpi. Granted, I could go much bigger, but this tends to be a good resolution when scanning objects with distinct edges. (See Figures 10.23 and 10.24.)

Figure 10.23 Scan at a high resolution.

Figure 10.24 Freshly picked leaf

Before we turn the leaf into a preset, let's separate it from the background. We could do this with Paths, as shown earlier in the book, but because the background is stark white and the leaf has crisp edges, we can simply use the Color Selection feature to select the background:

1. Choose Select → Color Range.
2. Click on the white area around the leaf.

Figure 10.25 Use Color Selection to select the white background.

Figure 10.26 Convert the background to a standard editable layer.

Figure 10.27 Look, Mom. I cleaned the background!

3. Hold down the Shift key, and select any areas of shadow around the leaf as well (Figure 10.25).
4. Double-click the Background layer, and convert it into a standard layer (Figure 10.26).
5. Hit Command/Control+A to select all the contents of the layer. Once selected, press Delete to wipe the white away (Figure 10.27).

The first preset we'll create is a custom shape. We'll need to delete all the shapes from the Custom Shape tool group:

1. Choose Edit → Presets.
2. Select Custom Shapes from the drop-down menu at the top.
3. Click on the first shape; then hold down the Shift key and click on the last shape in the set. This will select all the shapes in the group.
4. Click the Delete button to the right of the dialog box, and then click OK.

Now we need to create the leaf shape:

1. If your selection is still active, choose Select → Inverse. If not, simply ⌘/Ctrl-click the layer to generate the selection.
2. Go to the Paths panel. Click the Convert Selection To Path icon on the bottom of the panel.
3. Choose Edit → Define Custom Shape. Name the new leaf shape, and it is now available for your use in the Custom Shapes toolbox. (See Figure 10.28, 10.29, and 10.30.)

Figure 10.28 Convert the selection into a path.

Figure 10.29 Define and name the new leaf shape.

Figure 10.30 The leaf is now available for use in the Shapes toolbox.

You can now use the shape to create leaf patterns in any image you like. But wait… there's more! This leaf can now also be converted into a brush:

1. Create a new image. Any size will do, so long as the longest side is no bigger than 1200 pixels.
2. Draw your shape using green (Figure 10.31).
3. Rasterize the shape layer by choosing Layer → Rasterize → Layer (Figure 10.32).
4. You can now choose Edit → Define Brush Preset, name the new brush, and use the leaf brush as a painting tool (Figure 10.33).

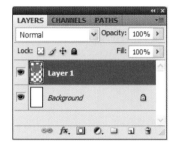

Figure 10.32 *Rasterize the shape layer.*

Figure 10.33 *Easily convert any shape into a brush.*

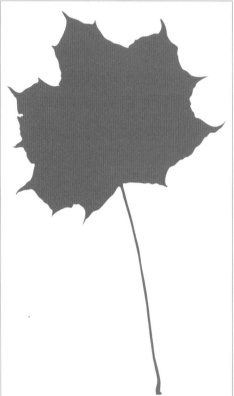

Figure 10.31 *You can now draw with the shape.*

That brush is fine if I just want a single color with no additional texturing or variation. But what if I want my brush to actually have those original leaf characteristics? Can a brush keep those tonal variations (in grayscale, at least) as the original scan? Definitely:

1. Return to the original scanned image.
2. Use the Eraser tool to wipe away most of the stem (Figure 10.34). Choose Image → Trim, and wipe away the excess areas around the leaf.

Figure 10.34 *Wipe away the stem with the Eraser tool.*

3. Resize the image, ensuring that the longest side is no more than 2500 pixels (Figure 10.35).

4. Choose Edit → Define Brush Preset. Name the brush and click OK (Figure 10.36).

You can now use this brush to paint with as well, and it will have all those little spots and tonal variations, texture, depth in the stem, and so on as you had in the original scan.

Now to give these presets a test run. Open the image `Fall.tif` (Figure 10.37) or any image you like. I picked this photo because of the falling leaves: They match up well with the presets just created.

Figure 10.35 *Resize the image.*

Figure 10.36 *Name and define the brush.*

Figure 10.37 *Winter is on the way.*

I'm not going to physically walk you through a design at this point. I simply want to give you an idea of what you can do with the tools you make. For instance, tools such as themed brushes and shapes are extremely popular among digital scrapbookers when designing their photo layouts and scrapbook pages. If you have never tried scrapbooking, I highly recommend it. Personally I find it to be very relaxing.

Okay, back to the image. In the following step, all I've done is to use the new custom shape to draw the leaf in a new layer. I then added a type selection and deleted it so the leaves in the photo could be seen, applied a fall-colored gradient with Layer Styles (Figure 10.38), and reduced the opacity of the layer to render it slightly transparent (Figure 10.39).

Figure 10.38 Fall tones in a gradient

Figure 10.39 Using the leaf to display the title

You can bring the brushes into the mix by using them to add a type of border or corner effect. You can set up the brush dynamics as shown in Chapter 8, "Going Beyond Canned Filters," to add texture, rotation, and size variations while you paint, and even variations in color (Figure 10.40). Adding a white layer with the opacity reduced creates a vellum effect and allows the brushed-on leaves to stand out a bit more (Figure 10.41).

So are we finished with the leaf? Not quite yet. You can also turn the leave texture into a seamless pattern and use it to apply to all sorts of things. In Figure 10.42 I've taken a sample of the leaf's interior. By using a series of masks and layer merges (Figure 10.43), I can create a seamless pattern (Figure 10.44), choose Edit → Define Pattern, name it (Figure 10.45), and use it with my Layer Styles.

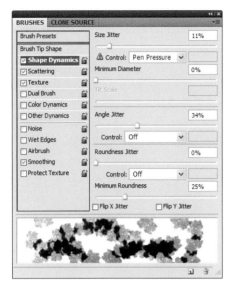

Figure 10.40 *Adjusting the brush characteristics*

Figure 10.41 *Painting with leaves*

Figure 10.42 *Sample the leaf texture.*

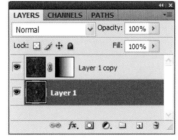

Figure 10.43 *Create a seamless pattern with masks and layer merges.*

Figure 10.44 *A new pattern emerges.*

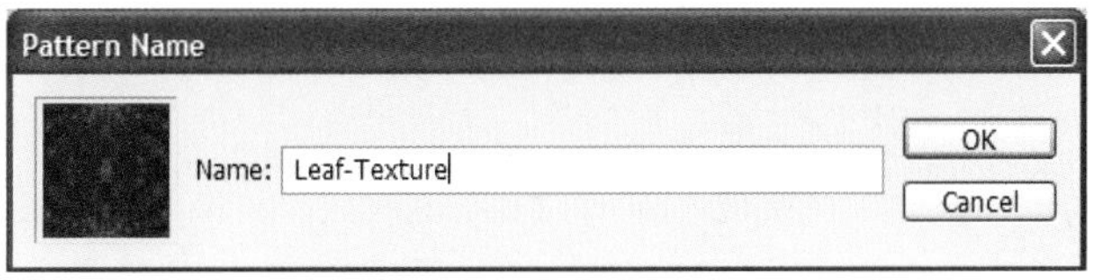

Figure 10.45 *Define the pattern.*

Now I can add that pattern into the design to give some texture to the original leaf shape. In order for the pattern to be visible, I'll need to open the styles for the leaf layer again and select the Gradient Overlay setting. By changing the blending mode of the Gradient Overlay to Soft Light, Photoshop will allow the Pattern Overlay (which resides beneath the Gradient Overlay in the Styles structure) to be visible (Figure 10.46).

Next I'll switch to Pattern Overlay, track down the freshly defined leaf pattern, and add it to the styles (Figure 10.47). The end result is a subtle application of the leaf texture to the leaf-shape layer (Figure 10.48).

For a parting shot I want to show you what the leaf pattern looks like on a repeating document. You can do some pretty interesting designs simply by manipulating texture photos (Figure 10.49).

I walked through this little demonstration to show you a few possibilities for turning your photos into presets you can use in other designs. When you look at Photoshop CS4 in this manner, you can actually salvage even the most abysmal photos and turn them into something constructive rather than instantly throwing them into the Recycle Bin. Nearly every photo, blurry or otherwise, has a tonal variety, a texture, or some other characteristic that can be used to generate tools for other aspects of your work.

Now on to the final segment of this chapter: how to turn people into monsters using a few simple adjustment layers (and a little dodging).

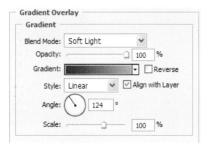

Figure 10.46 *Change the Gradient Overlay Blend Mode setting.*

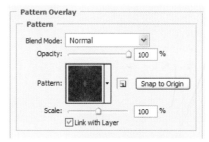

Figure 10.47 *Apply the Pattern Overlay.*

Figure 10.48 *Subtle texture in place*

Figure 10.49 *Repeating leaf pattern*

Project 3: Little Monsters

In nearly all of my books I try to pay homage to one of my favorite genres of design: dark art. *Dark* is a relative term, granted. Images filled with gore or the semblance thereof hold no interest for me. What I do enjoy are images that provoke an emotional response, so when I'm creating digital art for myself, I try to achieve just that.

This last section demonstrates how to alter the emotion, or *feel*, of a portrait with just a few quick tweaks. I'm using a portrait of a model in this instance, but you can easily achieve the same general emotion from a personal photo or a landscape scene (I did something similar with a graveyard project earlier in the book). The photo choice is up to you, and the level of alteration is up to your imagination and ability. You'll find that personal photos will render the best emotional response, simply because you are intimate with the subject or scene and know what you are trying to convey.

Open the image `Lefty.tif` (Figure 10.50). Since there will be some layer editing, duplicate the Background layer so that you have one to perform adjustments on in a couple steps:

1. Select the Background copy layer.
2. Choose Image → Adjustments → Hue/Saturation. Decrease the Brightness to –15 and increase the Contrast to 25 (Figure 10.51).
3. Click OK.

Let's do some work on the eyes. In this instance we don't need to recolor to get that evil look, as applying Dodge to brown tones lightens them to a red/orange:

1. Select the Dodge tool.
2. On the Options bar apply the following settings (Figure 10.52):

Brush	Round, Feathered, 40px
Range	Midtones
Exposure	50%
Protect Tones	Checked

3. Now apply the Dodge tool to the iris around the pupil to brighten the pixels, giving a sinister glow to the orb.
4. Since the Dodge tool is set to Midtones, the black in the pupil won't be altered. Just move the brush around in a circle pattern until you get a glow similar to that in Figure 10.53.

Figure 10.50 Half a portrait, ready for altering

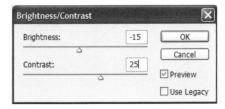

Figure 10.51 Decrease Brightness, increase Contrast.

Figure 10.52 Dodge-tool options

Figure 10.53
Sinister inner fire

From this point a series of adjustment layers will render the effect I'm looking for. To begin I'll start with the Channel Mixer. On the bottom of the Layers panel select Add An Adjustment Layer, and select Channel Mixer. Use the following settings (Figure 10.54):

Output Channel	Gray
Monochrome	Checked
Red	+40%
Green	+40%
Blue	+58%
Constant	–35%

Select Add An Adjustment Layer again, and this time select Photo Filter from the list. In the Adjustments panel enter the following settings (Figure 10.55):

Filter	Warming Filter (81)
Density	25%
Preserve Luminosity	Checked

Now we'll add another Channel Mixer layer. Create a new Channel Mixer adjustment layer with the following setting (Figure 10.56):

Channel Mixer	Black & White With Red Filter (RGB)

The effect on the image thus far should be a stark black-and-white effect. Now select the Paintbrush tool and choose Black as the foreground color. With a small, soft-feathered brush, paint over the iris areas in all three adjustment-layer masks to reveal the dodging done earlier in the process. The effect we are looking for can be seen in Figure 10.57.

Now simply apply more contrast to the image. You can do this with a Curves adjustment layer. Create a Curves adjustment layer at the top of the layer stack with a curve similar to that shown in Figure 10.58. I zoomed in to show the effect in the eye (Figure 10.59), and the final overall image is shown in Figure 10.60. You'll note that the lips have a bit of color in the final shot. I did this by painting with black in the layer mask of the first Channel Mixer layer. I think it adds just a bit more character to the final image.

Figure 10.54 *Channel Mixer #1*

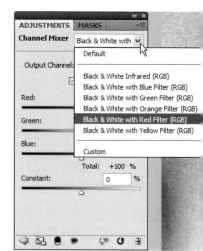

Figure 10.55 *Photo Filter*

Figure 10.56 *Channel Mixer #2*

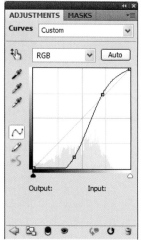

Figure 10.57 *Revealing the eye color once again*

Figure 10.58 *A final adjustment, this time with Curves*

Figure 10.59 *The final eye in close-up*

So what are we left with? Well, I'd say the model looks like a vampire. Quite a bit different from the original photo, wouldn't you say?

As you can see from this technique, not all extreme digital manipulations need be extreme in the process of getting from A to Z. Occasionally it takes only a few simple adjustments rather than a long, drawn-out process to alter the drama in a photo. Here we were able to achieve a dark effect with the use of three adjustment layers and a little dodging. As I mentioned before, try this on photos of yourself or your loved ones. You'll be amazed at the emotion you can get from simple alterations such as this.

Parting Thoughts

That's it for this book, my friends. I hope you have enjoyed this look into the right side of our collective brains. It is my sincere hope that you have learned something along the way and that you have been inspired to explore your creativity with this wonderful software.

Remember this: if you can imagine it, chances are Photoshop CS4 can help you realize it. The process of using your imagination in conjunction with the software can yield some very cool results, and often you'll find that simply experimenting with no end result in mind will open entirely new avenues of thought and creativity. You can't reach the top if you don't climb the hill. Remind yourself every time you open the program that Photoshop is simply a tool to enhance your vision. Keep it fun, and you'll be creating your own digital art in no time.

Figure 10.60 *The final image in full*

Appendices

APPENDIX

Accessing Additional Resources

It's been said that no matter *how much you know about Photoshop, you never stop learning more. To help guide your further explorations of the software, here are some of the most valuable online resources.*

The Manufacturer's Site

For all the latest in Adobe's software releases and technology, check out the source of it all: `http://www.adobe.com/products/photoshop/photoshop/`

Information and Discussion Sites

ActionFx Photoshop Resources (`www.actionfx.com`) The author's website. A vast resource for Photoshop training and custom add-ons for the software, including actions, layer styles, brushes, and so on. A large Free area and a huge Members area give access to thousands of custom-made Photoshop goodies and to training information.

PhotoshopCAFE (`www.photoshopcafe.com`) A website run by award-winning author and trainer Colin Smith. Tutorials, reviews, and more. Also one of the best Photoshop forums online. Stop in and say hello; I'll be lurking somewhere.

The Hidden Power of Photoshop Elements (`www.hiddenelements.com`) Author Richard Lynch's excellent website. Not only is Richard a qualified expert in Photoshop, but his talents have helped to unlock incredible features for Elements users also.

Digital Mastery (`www.digitalmastery.com`) If I had to recommend one person on this planet above all the other Photoshop gurus out there for in-depth training and understanding of the program, Ben Willmore would instantly come to mind. Ben is one of the most sought-after teachers in the field, and I highly recommend checking out his website and getting on his mailing list. You definitely will not regret it. 'Nuf said.

Photoshop Groups and Organizations

National Association of Photoshop Professionals (NAPP) (www.photoshopuser.com) The premier organization for Photoshop users around the globe, founded by Scott Kelby, renowned author and editor in chief of *Photoshop User* and *Layers* magazines. Although NAPP charges an annual membership fee, it is well worth the price for any serious Photoshop professional. I write for the website, so drop me a line when you visit.

Planet Photoshop (www.planetphotoshop.com)   Also operated by the team at NAPP, Planet Photoshop is a free resource for Photoshop users everywhere. Tutorials (many by yours truly), discounts, and resources abound; come check it out!

Adobe Photoshop Tutorials Online

PS Workshop (http://psworkshop.net)   When people ask me how to create a specific effect or where to find tutorials on a technique, this is the website I recommend. As of this writing, there are more than 1,700 tutorials linked to this site—definitely one for the books.

TeamPhotoshop (www.teamphotoshop.com)   Tutorials, forum, actions, resources galore—by people who love what they do and do what they love. Thanks for an excellent website!

Photoshop Top Secret (www.photoshoptopsecret.com)   You like effects? This guy knows effects! Mark Monciardini has been around longer than I have in this biz, and he remains at the top of his game in the Photoshop world. His website is ultracool; be sure to check out his new training videos. Mark is a designer's designer, is innovative in his tutorials, and has the unique ability to teach others and make learning fun as well as informative.

Stock Images

Stock photography websites, while not free, are great resources for designers who are seeking to increase the professional level of their work. Many of these resources offer complete access to low-, medium-, and high-resolution versions of their photos, taken by professional photographers.

Some of the websites listed here allow members to download the images online, others offer their photos on CD, and a couple give you both options. There are even some free ones to choose from. If you have a high-speed Internet connection, membership is probably more appealing because you do not have to wait for your photos; those of you with slow Internet connections may want to save on download time and opt for the CDs.

When you pay for a service, chances are you can get the resolution and professionalism that will make your work shine. Free resources, while they have their place, simply don't hold up to the quality that the paid sites offer. Free resources are generally operated by people who, while they have a passion for the photography, are not generating income from their website and must keep the image files small to save on bandwidth. Paid sites are set up so that bandwidth is not usually a concern, and they offer great service for those who choose their products.

Photos.com (www.photos.com)   One of many excellent resources operated by Jupiterimages, this site has a vast amount of stock photography available for download by its members. Most of the images in this book are from this great resource.

PhotoSpin (www.photospin.com)   This website offers to members over 100,000 images to download, as of this writing. Another excellent online repository for high-quality photography.

Clipart.com (www.clipart.com)   Also run by Jupiterimages, this website offers over 6 million downloadable images (clip art, photography, animations, and so on) to subscribers.

Getty Images (www.gettyimages.com)   A vast resource for professional photographs, including Time & Life Pictures and National Geographic. Categories include creative, editorial, film, custom imaging, and media management.

Comstock Images (www.comstock.com)   Specializes in commercial stock photography for advertising, graphic design, corporate marketing, publishing/desktop publishing, and web design. Offers royalty-free images that may be purchased individually or grouped on a CD.

Jupiterimages (www.jupiterimages.com)   Offers hundreds of thousands of images, free low-resolution comps, and high-resolution downloads. As of this writing, PictureQuest has nearly 500,000 images available.

Wetzel & Company (www.wetzelandcompany.com)   Offers background, pattern, and photographic texture images on CD.

AbleStock.com (www.ablestock.com)   Over 100,000 royalty-free digital images in three file sizes available to members for download.

iStockphoto (www.istockphoto.com)   Offers over 83,000 royalty-free files for members.

Free Stock Images

Stock.XCHNG (www.sxc.hu/)   An excellent resource for those on a budget looking for good-quality images for free. Browse, share, chat, and even access some excellent tutorials.

morgueFile (www.morguefile.com/)   Another wonderful resource to share photos with your peers or to enhance your image database.

B

About the Companion CD

In this appendix:

What you'll find on the CD

System requirements

Using the CD

Troubleshooting

What You'll Find on the CD

The following sections are arranged by category and provide a summary of the items you'll find on the CD.

Chapter Files

You will find images for you to use to practice the techniques in the book. They are arranged by chapter. Use them to follow along with the instructions and to try each new technique as it is presented. Taking the time to use these images will reinforce what you're reading.

For updates to any of the CD material, go to www.sybex.com/go/rightbrain.

System Requirements

The techniques in the book are geared primarily for users of Adobe Photoshop CS4 for Macintosh or Windows. Some of the techniques shown are applicable to previous versions of the software. Go to www.adobe.com for further information on system requirements for Photoshop. There is no software available on this CD.

Using the CD

To copy the items from the CD to your hard drive, follow these steps.

1. Insert the CD into your computer's CD-ROM drive. The license agreement appears.

Windows users: The interface won't launch if you have autorun disabled. In that case, click Start → Run (for Windows Vista, Start → All Programs → Accessories → Run). In the dialog box that appears, type **D:\Start.exe**. (Replace *D* with the proper letter if your CD drive uses a different letter. If you don't know the letter, see how your CD drive is listed under My Computer.) Click OK.

Mac users: The CD icon will appear on your desktop; double-click the icon to open the CD, and double-click the Start icon.

---

2. Read through the license agreement, and then click the Accept button if you want to use the CD.

The CD interface appears. The interface allows you to access the content with just one or two clicks.

Troubleshooting

Wiley has attempted to provide programs that work on most computers with the minimum system requirements. Alas, your computer may differ, and some programs may not work properly for some reason.

The two likeliest problems are that you don't have enough memory (RAM) for the programs you want to use, or you have other programs running that are affecting installation or running of a program. If you get an error message such as "Not enough memory" or "Setup cannot continue," try one or more of the following suggestions and then try using the software again:

Turn off any antivirus software running on your computer. Installation programs sometimes mimic virus activity and may make your computer incorrectly believe that it's being infected by a virus.

Close all running programs. The more programs you have running, the less memory is available to other programs. Installation programs typically update files and programs; so if you keep other programs running, installation may not work properly.

Have your local computer store add more RAM to your computer. This is, admittedly, a drastic and somewhat expensive step. However, adding more memory can really help the speed of your computer and allow more programs to run at the same time.

Customer Care

If you have trouble with the book's companion CD-ROM, please call the Wiley Product Technical Support phone number at (800) 762-2974. Outside the United States, call +1(317) 572-3994. You can also contact Wiley Product Technical Support at http://sybex .custhelp.com. John Wiley & Sons will provide technical support only for installation and other general quality-control items. For technical support on the applications themselves, consult the program's vendor or author.

To place additional orders or to request information about other Wiley products, please call (877) 762-2974.

Index

Index

Note to the Reader: Throughout this index boldfaced page numbers indicate primary discussions of a topic. Italicized page numbers indicate illustrations.